CHRIS JOHNSTON

Chris Johnston is a writer and theatre-maker whose work has spanned several art forms and many social constituencies. A formal list of positions would include directorships of arts organisations, while the informal would recognise working with groups of many kinds from apprentice witches to classical

DRAMA GAMES is a series of books for teachers, workshop leaders and directors in need of new and dynamic activities when working with actors in education, workshop or rehearsal.

Also in this series:

**DRAMA GAMES
FOR CLASSROOMS AND WORKSHOPS**
Jessica Swale

DRAMA GAMES FOR DEVISING
Jessica Swale

And more to follow…

The publisher welcomes suggestions for further titles in the series.

Chris Johnston

drama games
FOR THOSE WHO
LIKE TO SAY NO

Foreword by Ken Livingstone

NICK HERN BOOKS
London
www.nickhernbooks.co.uk

A Nick Hern Book

DRAMA GAMES
FOR THOSE WHO LIKE TO SAY NO

First published in Great Britain in 2010
by Nick Hern Books Limited
The Glasshouse, 49a Goldhawk Road,
London W12 8QP

Reprinted 2011, 2012 (twice)

Cover designed by www.energydesignstudio.com
Typeset by Nick Hern Books, London
Printed and bound in Great Britain by
Ashford Colour Press, Gosport, Hampshire

A CIP catalogue record for this book
is available from the British Library

ISBN   978 1 84842 049 6

For Luke

'Our big tough leader, away he wails
He thinks he is the kingpin but he's outraced
by that weedy little stranger with the grin on his face.'
Robin Williamson

FOREWORD

In the early 1980s, when the GLC (Greater London Council) was trying to save and create jobs to mitigate the impact of Thatcher's recession, we discovered that the most labour-intensive form of public spending was the arts, and so during the five years from 1981 to 1986 we increased spending on arts and recreation from £16 million to £160 million. Virtually every actor, painter, poet, sculptor and, in particular, community artist was in work, and it made London a much more exciting city to live in. As well as taking orchestras from the Royal Festival Hall to play in the canteen at Ford's Assembly Plant in Dagenham, we particularly tried to reach disaffected youth. It's against that background that I was able to understand Chris Johnston's book. (Oh, and by the way, if you want to know which is the least labour-intensive form of public spending, it is the military.)

Tragically, the casualties of Thatcher's assault on the public sector in 1980 are still with us today, as are their children and now their grandchildren: three generations of the same family who have never known a secure job. Towns and communities, as well as whole industries, were devastated and many have never recovered. We see the consequences in the levels of illiteracy, crime, drug addiction and alcoholism. David Cameron talks about a 'broken Britain', and yes, it is, in parts, but he doesn't have the courage to tell us who broke it or that the policies of his government are going to repeat those tragic errors and create another generation of casualties. There will be such a demand for people like Chris Johnston and his work; it could be the only growth industry we have under this present government.

If we are to heal the individuals and the communities who have been excluded and left behind, we need to recognise the vital role that the arts can play in regenerating communities and engaging young people, and Chris's work should be the sourcebook for inspiration and strategies to achieve this.

It's an electrifying experience to watch drama engaging people who have experienced nothing but powerlessness in their lives. Because it's accessible it offers a language by which young people can bring their anger to the surface. Since this country followed America down the path of doubling our prison population, drama is one of the few things that can bring a humanising influence, dialogue and learning into our prisons, giving prisoners the chance to escape the deadening experience that our under-resourced prison service offers them.

Chris's work empowers young people by relying on *them* rather than teachers to find a role that allows them to express their anger, escape their alienation and help see the creative capacity in themselves and those around them. This book offers invaluable ways for artists, teachers, workshop leaders and activists to better use the arts to empower young people and reduce social exclusion.

Ken Livingstone
London, August 2010

Ken Livingstone is a broadcaster and Labour Party politician. He was Leader of the Greater London Council from 1981 to 1986, MP for Brent East from 1987 to 2001, and London's first elected Mayor from 2000 to 2008.

CONTENTS

Foreword by Ken Livingstone   *vii*

Introduction   *xv*
Shaking Hands with Difficulty

Acknowledgements   *xxix*

Part One – ENGAGEMENT

1.	Name Three Times	2
2.	Football Teams	3
3.	Identifying Objects	4
4.	Passing the Object	5
5.	Newspaper Race	6
6.	The Chairs Game	7
7.	Bomb and Shield	8
8.	Yes / No	9
9.	Numbers Game	10
10.	Numbers Game 2	11
11.	Hiss and Boo	12
12.	Bang!	13
13.	Drama Nein Danke	14
14.	Ailments	15
15.	Continuum	16
16.	Tin-Can Pulse	17
17.	Dog and Bone	18
18.	The Don	19
19.	Working with Images	20
20.	The Scarf Game	21
21.	Prisoner's Dilemma	22

Part Two – PLAY

22.	No, You Didn't	24
23.	Complete the Image	25
24.	Antiques	26
25.	Changeable Object	27
26.	Vampires	28
27.	Shoes Game	29
28.	The Bears are Coming	30
29.	Cat and Mouse	31
30.	Zoom – Screech	32
31.	Staring Competition	33
32.	Word Smuggling	34
33.	Wizards, Giants, Elves	35
34.	Russian Shoemakers	36
35.	The Egg Game	37

Part Three – COLLABORATION

36.	Tug of War	40
37.	On the Bus	41
38.	Map of the Town	42
39.	Clint Eastwood	43
40.	Body Map	44
41.	The Identity Zone	45
42.	The Truth About Drugs and Crime	46
43.	Hunting the Lion	47
44.	Newspaper Game	48

Part Four – SKILLS

Observation

45.	Kim's Game	52
46.	The Behaviour of the Room	53
47.	Find Your Gang	54
48.	The Big Picture	55
49.	Bandleader	56
50.	Whose Story is True?	57

Reasoning

51.	Predicaments	60
52.	Press-Ups	61
53.	Shortest Time Possible	62
54.	Name That Object	63
55.	Obstacle Race	64
56.	Missing Character	65
57.	What Happened Here?	66
58.	Priorities	67
59.	The Balloon	68
60.	Gossip	69

Kinaesthetic

61.	Boxing	72
62.	Sticks	73
63.	Shapes in the Dark	74
64.	Journeys	75
65.	Fast-Food Martial Arts	76
66.	Lightest Point of Contact	77

Communication

67.	The Argument Game	80
68.	I'm a Celebrity Prisoner, Get Me Out of Here!	81
69.	Word Smuggling 2	82
70.	Animals / Drink / Sport	83
71.	Minefield	84
72.	Chinese Mime	85
73.	The Argument Room	86
74.	Community Centre	87

Negotiation

75.	Taxi Ride	90
76.	The Jobsworth Line	91
77.	Both Want the Car	92
78.	Blue Room, Green Room	93
79.	The Wedding Funeral	94
80.	Drunk on the Bus	95
81.	Three Nations	96

Performance

82.	Reactions	*100*
83.	Following	*101*
84.	Two People Meet	*102*
85.	First Lines of Scenes	*104*
86.	Blind Offers	*106*
87.	The Bridge	*108*
88.	Park Bench	*110*
89.	Two Rush In	*111*
90.	Selling	*112*

Part Five – CHALLENGES

Mediation Skills

91.	The Stolen Jacket	*120*
92.	The Chat-Up	*122*
93.	The Old People's Home	*124*
94.	Forged Tickets	*126*
95.	The Couple Who Argue	*128*

Communication Skills

96.	The Chairs	*132*
97.	The Christmas Present	*134*
98.	The Youth Club	*136*
99.	The Untrustworthy Partner	*138*
100.	Cold Turkey	*140*

Negotiation Skills

101.	The Job Centre	*142*
102.	The Burger Bar	*144*
103.	The Post Office	*146*
104.	Drugs in Prison	*148*
105.	The Mobile Phone Shop	*150*

Assertiveness

106.	Carpets by Moonlight	*154*
107.	Bullying at Work	*156*
108.	Taking Care of Grandpa	*158*
109.	The Fire Station	*160*
110.	Talking to the School	*162*

Managing Emotions

111. The Broken Radio   *164*
112. The Adult Education Class   *166*
113. The Bully Boyfriend   *168*
114. Zone of Confrontation   *170*
115. Mistaken Identity   *172*

Part Six – TRAINING

116. Pushing   *176*
117. Brilliant / Shit   *183*
118. A New National Flag   *187*
119. Ladder of Engagement   *191*

Index of Games

Keywords   *196*
Alphabetical List   *205*

INTRODUCTION

Shaking Hands with Difficulty

This is a book about using drama with so-called difficult groups.

That is, groups that might be characterised as awkward, resistant, rebellious, intransigent, problematic or simply out for a good time when that means a good time at others' expense. Groups, in other words, of probably younger men or women who take great pleasure in saying 'no' to whatever is offered them. For these players, games need to be pretty robust in their structure; both fun to play and engaging. They need to hook in the participants using activity that's exciting, challenging or subversive.

The book is structured in progressive chapters, each containing a series of games and exercises. First up is a selection of games that are about Engagement; these help to enlist the participants into activity. These are what you might use when you first walk in the room or after you've negotiated issues of behaviour. Such exercises would be characterised by an easy set of rules, the avoidance of any harsh spotlight on participants, and possibly a competitive element.

When the group's behaviour suggests it's ready for more creative activity, structures can be introduced that rely less on competition and more on inventiveness. So the next section is about Play. Games in this section can fall apart if the group is still resistant to anything non-competitive, so it's best to get beyond that point first. We're entering a Lewisian wardrobe into a world of imagination. Young people are often reluctant to confess to having an imagination, as if in some way that acknowledgement might leave them open to arrest.

But this suspicion that admitting to imagination will lead to personal humiliation probably has its origins not in the perception of theatre as some life-threatening disease, but rather the culture of home life. The toxic fear of creativity may well be a consequence of living in an atmosphere of conflict and hostility, where ridicule is the norm. So they cheerfully bring all that along to the session.

Then we move on to Collaboration when it seems that, yes, the group is ready to achieve that. This means working together on tasks that call for inter-group communication and a willingness to sacrifice personal enthusiasms in favour of a consensus view. Exercises are creative for the most part, but do borrow some elements from the worlds of strategy-planning and sport.

The following and largest section is on Skills, and this breaks down into subsections. The word 'skill' can sometimes imply a sedentary or industrial activity, but it doesn't have to be that. The word 'workshop' is problematic enough, implying metal, wood and lathes being hammered together in an out-of-town industrial estate. However, the business that's going on here is pretty different, allied instead to a notion that the traditional division between work and play doesn't actually have to exist. There's a somewhat depressing tradition that anyone 'having to go to work' should be consoled with 'oohs' and 'ahs' of sympathy, just as 'going off work' is greeted with smiling and cheery banter. It probably comes from a period when most work was back-breaking and something akin to slave labour, only with (modest) pay. And of course plenty of that is still around. In this context, the 'work time = bad, free time = good' set of equations do kind of work. But in the cultural industries, we don't have to subscribe to those equations, and in fact we do bolshily argue against their hegemony. All the best things about 'time off' have here been captured for work (playfulness, imagination and mucking about), and all the bad things about 'time in work' (heaving a pick or stacking shelves) have been left out. Okay, it's not achieved every time, but the intent is there.

Each subsection in Skills deals with a different aptitude that could be useful for those who are unproductively at odds with society. Some exercises are creative and some are about communication and social skills, but the spirit powering all of them remains the same: playfulness and spontaneity, freedom of imagination and a rough-hewn democracy.

Next up is Challenges. These are somewhat different; not games or exercises as such, but a range of scenarios written and created for individuals to test out their social skills. The scenario is usually prepared with the facilitators and the participating group while the key player, the challenger, is out of the room. He or she has then to come into the room, be told about the governing fiction, be given a task or objective, and then deal with any conflicts or problems that arise within that fiction as it is acted out. Exercises of this kind are often called role plays or simulations. The scenarios presented here were all developed by me with colleagues such as Saul Hewish and Richmond Trew of Rideout for use in prison or probation contexts. To implement these requires a certain amount of time spent in the set-up. It also usually means involving others in the group to play roles. More information is given in the chapter's preamble.

Finally, there are Training exercises; how to get fit before you enter the arena of combat. These are for use by facilitators away from the difficult group and are not to be replicated there; the purpose is training, pure and simple. I developed these when I was asked to train other facilitators in dealing with resistance. It surprised me to be asked since I'd never seen it as separable from the business of making theatre in unlikely contexts, but it did present a good opportunity to break down just what that notion actually implied. I would happily admit that there can be little substitute for launching yourself into a real-life situation with a colleague and trying out some ideas where meanings are blurred and the legitimacy of your role is always in question. But just as trainee teachers discover when they finally hit the classroom that although absorption of theory does not a warrior make for the new society, it does give you a rucksack containing some useful weapons; so too, training in running drama workshops has its place.

Ground Plans

Inevitably we have to imagine a certain kind of group for whom these games and exercises are suitable. But I'm deliberately leaving this a bit vague. You the reader can take a look at what's here and make your own decision about which exercise is right for your group. But we're clearly talking about groups to be found outside professional arts contexts. We're thinking about closed institutions, hospitals, probation centres, youth clubs, schools and holiday schemes.

The book could have been arranged in the form of games for different groups. Chapters would be headed 'Exercises for young people' and 'Exercises for older young people' and so on, but this might have become a little tortuous. We'd have ended up with 'Exercises for young people who have a drugs problem, have missed out on education and follow football but hate Arsenal and are on supervision attending a summer school'. So instead I went for categorisation according to the function of the game. The exercises range quite widely in terms of the challenge they present to any group taking them on. Some will be effective in many situations; some will work well only in a few. Many of the exercises simply won't work at all for those in wheelchairs, but there are others that will. Overall, there are many that I've invented, but many too – perhaps the majority in the earlier chapters – that I've borrowed and possibly altered. Given that so much of my own personal experience has been in prison or probation contexts, much of the content will reflect this.

Of course, you don't usually just walk into a room and kick-start a game. There's a range of issues that need to be addressed before any moving, jumping, pushing or swearing actually takes place. But given that this tome is in the unreliable but essentially honourable tradition of games books, not a lot of time will be spent on the planning issues or the philosophy around the value of games. But we can't spend no time at all, lest that implies the pre-work isn't important. And as those in the know know, it very much is.

To make it brief, let's set out some of the main considerations that have to be looked at before any community arts project, such as a drama workshop series, begins. Because we're treading into a territory where social science and the arts have become hitched – a marriage made in helium that can breed misunderstandings faster than a superconductor – it's necessary to be pretty clear about how to conceptualise the practice. You can actually break down all the issues pertaining to community arts, at least in respect of project management, into three broad categories:

- Context
- Objective
- Strategies

If anyone has found an issue that can't be considered under those headings, let me know. I've been throwing out the challenge for a few years and nobody's come back yet.

The context category is really all about everything that isn't the work itself. It breaks down into two further subsections: the human and the environmental. The human element refers to the nature of the group; its size, composition, place in any hierarchy and the codes or values that underpin its working. Has the group worked together before? Does it have awareness of itself as a group? Are the members of the group obliged to be present or is this a voluntary project? What are their expectations, if any? What are the expectations of those in authority over them? What do the men and women in the big upstairs want out of this project? Avoid this question at your peril. Do members of the group have any kind of special needs, and if so, how are those needs going to be met during the project? Answers to all these questions, if obtained and absorbed by the workshop leaders, will put the team in a great position come the first day of working. They represent valuable information that will help to make decisions around the other two key elements: objective(s) and strategies.

The second part of the context is the environment. Where will the sessions be held? Is it an appropriate venue? Are there any health or safety issues arising? If the venue isn't suitable, it's better not to run the session at all. One important consideration is the floor. Any surface that is very hard like concrete or very soft like a downy carpet will immediately restrict the range of activities. Much of this is common sense. Similarly, if there are interesting but non-usable objects or strange items of furniture in the room, they may provide an unwelcome distraction. I was once asked to run a session in a prison room with acupuncture chairs. Great for lying back on and doing bugger all in.

The context determines what's possible. The objective sets down a marker for what you want to achieve within that context. It's also something of a beacon in the night. When you get lost, feeling that all around you are losing their heads, including you, it's good to think back in a moment of calm, if you can find it, and remember just why you started the project. And it is very easy to get lost, especially if things move off in a mayhem direction. Those who can't punt back from this vortex of failure are often those who misunderstand the difference between strategies and objectives.

Sometimes people assume, for example, that 'making a play' is an objective. Well, it is and it isn't. You make a play for a reason. Say, for example, you want to raise the profile of the group or help empower it in some way. Or perhaps you want to educate the group in what the art form can offer, or make a statement to an audience about something the group wants the audience to understand. So, for any one or more of these reasons, you make a play. The production, therefore, is clearly a strategy, perhaps the primary strategy, but nevertheless only a strategy in the task of pushing for a larger objective that's really about social development.

In the same way, you run a series of drama workshops not just to get to the end of them and walk away tired, exhilarated and absurdly pleased with yourself, but to do something else: to effect an experience that leaves the participants changed. The objective is usually about something beyond the immediate task.

This may be as blindingly obvious as the need for an oxygen supply when you go underwater, or the benefit of air travel to the international drug smuggler, but in terms of the kind of projects that we're talking about, it's pretty important to get right what your objective really is. If you can't do that, it's an inevitable outcome that choosing your strategies is going to be something of a hit-and-miss affair, akin to putting the tail on the donkey while wearing a blindfold after drinking several pints of beer. Besides, we're working in a time when so many previously well-established distinctions between art-form functions and intellectual disciplines are becoming increasingly unclear. Today the dividing lines between dance and theatre, training and performance, and social science and creative arts are just not there in the same way as they once were. You look down at your feet and the formerly neat lines have become crazy zigzags and looping circles. So intellectual and conceptual clarity about the project and your responsibility within it is no optional extra.

Coming to the issue of strategies, it's worth pointing out that there are both macro-strategies and micro-strategies. The macro would include the production, the text if there is one, the series of workshops or rehearsals, the use of a particular location and the team you've assembled for the project. The micro would be the individual games and exercises within any session. Digging even further down through the strata, we'd come to the small, moment-by-moment decisions you'd make as a facilitator in the room. I guess these would be the micro-micro or even microscopic strategies.

It's fairly self-evident then that congruence between the context, the objective and the strategies is pretty essential if you hope to pull off a successful project. If you mismatch this arrangement and work on Shakespeare's sonnets in an institution for violent juveniles with a graffiti artist, you might walk away feeling something other than exhilarated. Then again, you might just work a miracle. I wouldn't want to prejudge. Well, maybe I would…

The Team

As mentioned, the team created to run the project is also a key strategy in the game plan. Often individual practitioners make the mistake of thinking that they can go into a closed institution, hospital or youth centre and run a series of sessions *tout seul*. It's not that it can't be done but, generally speaking, this comes under the heading of 'Big Mistake' or possibly even 'Why Didn't Someone Stop Me?' All my big mess-ups were made without another facilitator present. There have been a few with other colleagues in the room as well, but the severity of my stupidity was at least partially checked. There's also, before getting in the room, someone to plan with and, after coming out, someone to share the review. Someone, in other words, who can bring fresh perspectives to the work at all stages. Where the client group is volatile, prone to infighting or simply lacking discipline, running the session on your own can reasonably be described as irresponsible not just in relation to yourself but to those who've trusted you with the gig. It's too easy to get into a self-defeating argument with someone who'd be happy to see the session disintegrate, and then not be able to walk away from it. The session can collapse faster than a dream on waking. I've seen it, and there really is a point of decomposition beyond which any return involves some kind of very unavailable magic.

It's also problematic if someone in the group becomes upset and you need to talk with them privately. It's hard to do that while still leading.

You're introducing a different, perhaps unfamiliar culture. Its elements of collaboration, democracy, non-discrimination and humility may well be resisted. You'll need allies in there with you.

So, back to building the team. You need a range of skills in that team much as Bob the Builder, as he likes to tell us with great emphasis, needs Wendy, Lofty and Co. If there aren't the skills, talent, passion and enthusiasm in some kind of balance, even though you have a team of a kind, you're starting from a position of weakness. If the team members don't complement each other in their skill areas, then you might be building a house extension with three plasterers and no electrician. Workshop leaders need to complement each other; to bring something different along, either as artists in different art forms or because they function differently: one is ideas and visions, another is method and application. One is fire, one is ice. One is physical contact and gregariousness, the other is intellectual distance. Team members also need to know how their roles differ when it comes to tasks and problems. And most importantly, the selection of a team needs to reflect an understanding of who the client group is. If possible, the gender and ethnicity determinants of the participant group need be reflected in the leadership team. This isn't a rule, of course, but when there's a big difference between the backgrounds of the two sides, then you need full confidence in your skill set to engage the group without those common factors helping the chemistry.

Reasons to Do

Ultimately, your objectives and strategies will reflect the values that you hold as an artist and citizen. If you are unclear about these, you become vulnerable to challenge. Why are you doing this work? It's an important question that may well be thrown at you. It'll probably come after the question about how much money you're earning and before the one about whether you've been on television. I know if I haven't got an answer, I start looking like the abseiling instructor who goes halfway down the cliff face in front of his students and runs out of rope. I guess for me there are answers I make available for public consumption, and then there are the private answers. The reasons I give when challenged, which are not dishonest, are about valuing the chance to create something extraordinary and unique with this group. Especially because this group, if it's the case, can come to performance without the baggage of professional techniques and create work that has a liveness and rawness about it. That's a welcome antidote to professional packaging with its emphasis on sensation. And besides, I find it good fun to bring my knowledge of dramatic structures into this context where it can be useful.

The more private reasons are less defined and perhaps more selfish. I guess they are about eating at a table that I would never otherwise get access to. Growing up in a family where self-expression was forbidden unless it chimed with a very bourgeois notion of acceptability, I was left hungry to champion the cause of anti-censorship and self-expression. Part of the reason might be to do with the fact that my father was empowered by the state to work as a theatre censor and happily sat watching the plays of Harold Pinter and Spike Milligan with a red pencil in his hand. (Actually, it was blue, he tells me.) I'd been overwhelmed and intoxicated by an experience of radical performance when I left home and wanted to get that experience validated by exporting it to others and enlisting them into its strangeness. I also wanted, being nosy by nature, to peer through other people's windows and shout, 'Hey, you could make a play about that', rather in the annoying way that drunks grab hold of you at parties and say the same.

I also feel instinctively that going to a very difficult place – and by 'place' I really mean situation – I'm confronted and challenged, and that could just be good for me. I hate acknowledging that, but it's true. Besides, I'm very much aware how inadequate my education was. Going into a difficult group and trying to lead it somewhere, while the experience can be draining and dispiriting at times, does probably in the end come out on the plus side in the balance sheet of life's less bonkers activities. Or so I believe, optimistically. It gives you a certain mettle. Or perhaps it's metal. If so, then its constituent elements are patience, understanding and resilience. My background was quite protected, as I say, even privileged, and given the terrible burden of not being beaten as a child or locked in a cupboard for weeks on end, it left me needing to go on something of a Conradian journey. Right now, that need is lessened not just because of the number of times I've been knocked off the boat, thrashed about in the water and had to wrestle sharks into writing poetry, but also because of the number of times I've made it up the river, got home and written up a log.

So back to the book. To repeat the point made at the beginning, the sections are set out in a way that can be seen as progressive, working from the simple to the more complex. Of course, there are many occasions where this notion of progress can and should be turned on its head. In this moment, a collaborative or challenge exercise is just the thing you're looking for to effect engagement. And what you need to conclude with is something from the Engagement section that's very simple indeed and allows everyone to let off steam. In such instances, circumstance needs to become the parent of principle. The cry of 'Oh, the session didn't work because the group weren't comfortable with my session plan' doesn't really hold up; you've got to be pragmatic and respond to exigencies – preferably without losing your moral compass.

Unguided Missiles

Every group in the world will have its own temperature, disposition and inclination. It's a matter of trying to understand these and use the group's own momentum to drive the engine of the event. No two groups will respond the same way to the same exercise. The best sessions almost always represent a revision of what you had planned.

What is easily forgotten when working with difficult groups is that you're very likely de facto an advocate for the arts themselves in a way you didn't anticipate. 'What's the point of this shit?' and 'What am I going to get out of this?' represent a second set of questions following on from those about your values, which are similarly difficult to answer. Why? Because the answers are bigger than China and you have about thirty seconds before some numpty kicks off. And you need to be in China or some such other place to answer the question, and right now you're in Kentucky or Birmingham, some place that's very far from China. So you do the best you can, relying on being candid and honest, and hoping that's sufficient. But it's not surprising that talking about the transformative power of art in an atmosphere of sullen petulance and muttering discontent can make you sound like an academic extolling the benefits of early Ken Dodd videos to the Taliban.

It helps not to underestimate the appeal of being an unguided missile. Saying no is an empowering act, one bestowing a satisfying and fulfilling sense of individuality. 'You in the herd over there, I'll have you know that I don't belong with you, I go my own way. So deal with it.' This is a powerful position to take. It gets the speaker attention from the whole room. Before long, the speaker is thinking, 'Now everyone has to work around me and my concerns. I don't necessarily know what those concerns are and probably wouldn't share them if I did but, hey, I'm running the show. Oh, so now the authority figure is starting to question me… but this works out too because I get a chance to make a statement proving that a logical, linear, empathic, problem-solving approach to the concerns I've just raised is simply inappropriate here. I think "Fuck off" might just do it.'

Nor is it a mistake to underestimate the appeal of provoking conflict in the room. Conflict is exciting, it's stimulating, it upsets the order of things. It creates drama (and isn't that why we're here?), helping me as a participant to externalise some of the stuff I'm feeling inside. 'Okay, these people aren't responsible for my feeling of desperation but that distinction is pretty irrelevant just now. At least if the conflict is out there rather than in here, then I'm getting confirmation of a basic truth, which is: life is pretty shitty, okay, and right now I've got some problems that can't be solved. And they certainly can't be solved by you.'

Yet the trusted instinct of the facilitator is to think, 'I can solve this. All we need is a different game.' Well, yes, maybe, but come to think of it, no. Alright, you can change your approach but it's possible this will make no difference at all. It may be better if that participant takes his or her anger for a walk.

Sometimes asking a participant to sit out and watch is a good alternative to arranging an escort out of the project. It works best if it's just one participant sitting out and watching. Once there's more than one, you won't necessarily have a quiet spectator; you'll have an alternative party. And that party won't be dedicated to the realisation of a holistic, democratic and egalitarian fulfilment of the creative potential of all the participants present.

When the suggestion is initially put, the participant may think that sitting out will be a great way to demonstrate outsider-ness. But sometimes the actual experience of sitting out is quite different. It's one of feeling excluded and wanting to be involved again. If this feeling develops, then the strategy is working and the participant should be brought back in. But it also may happen that the participant decides that sitting out is akin to being in the naughty corner, and asks to leave. But at least a positive strategy has been tried.

As suggested earlier, flexibility and a willingness to adapt principle to pragmatics without throwing the compass out of the window, usually presents as a good way to go. Ultimately, when shaking hands with difficulty, you have to go with your best instinct and make what feels like a bold decision. You never know, it might even be a good one.

Chris Johnston

ACKNOWLEDGEMENTS

My thanks go to Saul Hewish especially, also Richmond Trew, Bharti Patel, Fateha Begum, Sally Brookes, and all those others who've collaborated with me on this work. I'd also like thank Maggie Gordon-Walker, without whom the work would mean far less.

On the publication side, Matt Applewhite at Nick Hern Books has been tireless in bringing clarity where otherwise there would be muddle and opacity. Finally, there are many professionals working within a criminal justice environment who enabled projects which have allowed this work to be created. Of them, my particular thanks go to Trevor Laud and Pete Knapton. Oh yes, and all the participants: they had a fair bit to do with it as well.

Note on numbers of players and ages: *These are a very rough guide.*

Note on timings of games: *These assume a group of around eight players, but you should treat these timings with considerable suspicion!*

PART ONE

ENGAGEMENT

These games and exercises are about making the transition from social interaction to game-based interaction, while bringing as many as possible of the participants along.

ENGAGEMENT

Name Three Times

Moving from chat to game, no one even has to leave their seat.

How to Play

The group sit in a circle, on chairs.

The facilitator stands in the middle. There are no spare chairs.

He or she is trying to sit down. The way to do this is to say the first name of someone in the group as quickly as possible three times, before that person can say his or her own name once. If this is achieved, the facilitator or player in the centre sits in the chair of the person whose name was just called.

Now the player who has been deposed has to try and sit down, using the same technique.

If the person whose name was called does manage to say their name before it's been called three times, then the player in the centre has to try with someone else.

Benefits of the Game

Wakes everybody up.

Helps to bring everyone into a shared focus, a shared activity.

It also encourages players to accept a very simple, competitive set of rules, hopefully meaning that more elaborate game structures can be introduced later.

Players	Age	Time
Any number	10+	10

Football Teams

The mention of football can trigger a somewhat heated exchange; I've known participants simply refuse to play the game unless they can play under the colours of the team they support.

How to Play

Three football teams are chosen and everyone is assigned to one of the three teams.

The group sits in a circle, on chairs, all except for one player who remains in the middle. There needs to be good-sized spaces between the chairs.

The centre player wants to sit down but there are no more chairs. He or she calls out a name of one of the three teams. All the members of that team then have to change places.

As this is happening, the centre player tries to sit down. Whoever fails to get a chair after all are seated needs to stand in the middle and call a new team.

It's also possible for the centre player, instead of calling a team, may call 'Football League', in which case everyone has to move.

Benefits of the Game

Encourages attentiveness, speed of movement, sharpness of mind.

Variations and Extensions

Instead of using football teams, any category of people from sport or elsewhere might be used. The game might lead on to '*Anyone Who…*'. In this, the person in the centre defines a personal characteristic, which must apply to him or herself. For example, '*Anyone who has red hair/two legs/plays football/has been in a plane.*' Any player in the circle for whom this is true needs to get up and find a new chair. Once again, the centre player needs to sit down. It's vital that in '*Anyone Who…*' the characteristic is true of the person in the middle – otherwise the game is open to abuse or bullying.

Players	Age	Time
Any number	10+	10

Identifying Objects

Simple, hard to resist playing.

How to Play

Lay some small objects out on a table. Make sure that the majority of the objects are hard to identify, or a little unusual. Make sure that the players don't see the objects being laid out.

Ask for a volunteer and apply a blindfold.

The blindfolded player has to identify as many objects on the table as possible, through touch alone.

A new set of objects will be needed for the next player.

Benefits of the Game

Heightened sensitivity through touch, concentration, use of imagination.

Variations and Extensions

Use a black bag like photographers use for loading a film – or they used to, before digital kicked all that into touch. Put the objects in the black bag (it needs to have a closed neck so the objects can't be seen). Then ask each player, after he or she has 'felt' in the bag, to write down their object definitions.

Now it's clearly a competition as to who can identify the most objects. This variation means you don't have to change the objects for every new player.

+ Assorted small objects		
Players	**Age**	**Time**
Any number	10+	10

Passing the Object

The individual versus the team.

How to Play

Ask all the players apart from one to stand in a line, facing the same way. They need to stand close together.

The final player stands in front of the line.

An object is given to the players in the line.

These players pass the object between them by using their hands behind their backs.

The player in front has to work out where the object is at any one time.

This player calls out *'Stop!'* at any time. When this is done, other players have to stop moving the object behind them. (A facilitator may need to stand behind the line to check there is no cheating.)

Then the player calls out who they think has the object.

If the player calls correctly, he or she may change places with the player correctly called.

Benefits of the Game

Observation of body language, legitimation of light physical contact, communication skills, motor skills.

Variations and Extensions

The game could be played with the accumulation of points; in which case, if the call is correct that's one point to the player and none to the team. If the call is incorrect, that's one to the team and none to the player. It's a best of five.

+ Assorted small objects		
Players	**Age**	**Time**
Any number	10+	10

Newspaper Race

Haste is an enemy of care.

How to Play

This game works best in a large or at least a long space.

Organise two teams of equal number.

Provide each team with the same number of sheets of newspaper, probably two each.

Each team has to travel the length of the space without touching the floor, using only the newspaper.

The first to get to the other side is the winner.

It's possible to instruct that either the newspaper has to be kept as pristine as possible – or points are deducted for damage. *Or* you can do whatever you like with the newspaper. If the latter, it's probably better to have quite small pieces of newspaper otherwise the teams will move over the space too quickly.

Benefits of the Game

Teamwork, the cultivation of ingenuity, the generation of excitement.

Variations and Extensions

Run the game as a competition between pairs. Give each pair a cardboard box. The race is between the pairs. The rule is, you have to travel across the floor and back as a pair with only the box being allowed to touch the floor.

+ Newspaper, boxes		
Players	**Age**	**Time**
8+	10+	10

The Chairs Game

As long as the group is mobile, it never fails.

How to Play

Arrange the chairs randomly throughout the space (a large space is preferable). Each chair should be a similar distance from other chairs, and all should point in different directions.

Ask players to occupy a chair each, leaving one spare chair for the facilitator.

Instruct the players that they have to work together to prevent the facilitator from sitting down. Let's call the facilitator playing this role 'the outsider'. The only way the group is allowed to prevent the outsider from sitting down is by occupying the chairs. But if a player moves from his chair to the spare chair, then that initial chair is now free. So another player has to fill it.

Also explain that the outsider will give the group a chance to win by moving slowly, by shuffling along the floor, rather than running.

On the word '*Go*', the outsider heads for the free chair and the game is on. Players can move freely between the chairs but can't otherwise impede the travel of the outsider. Once the outsider has managed to sit down, the game can be repeated.

It may be useful to encourage the team to engage in tactical discussions between rounds.

Benefits of the Game

Teamwork, self-observation, management of impulses.

Note

Sometimes the game is played with different players taking the role of the outsider. Personally I'd discourage this. The game works best when the focus is on challenging the group to work together as a team.

Players	Age	Time
8+	10+	15

Bomb and Shield

What's amazing is the look on people's faces when they see how such a simple rule can create so much physical activity.

How to Play

Instruct each person to select someone from the group but to keep to themselves who they have selected. Then tell the group that that person selected is, to the chooser, a bomb.

Next, everyone must select a second person. That person will be a shield for the chooser.

On the word '*Go*', everyone should aim to achieve a physical position in the room where they are 'protected'. '*Find a position so that your shield is between you and the bomb.*'

Inevitably, everyone will be moving quickly around the room, trying to negotiate the ever-changing arrangement of bodies in the space.

There's an option to call out '*The bomb is going off in ten, nine, eight…*' etc., thereby raising the stakes.

Benefits of the Game

Observation, the cultivation of playfulness, the increase of energy and excitement, physical contact.

Variations and Extensions

To achieve a different kind of result, it's possible to interrupt the playing of the game in this way: while the players are running around, shout '*Freeze!*' Then pick one of the players and ask, for example: '*Look at this image you're in – what do you think might be going on here?*' You're asking for a response that imaginatively interprets the frozen action.

Players	Age	Time
8+	10+	5

Yes / No

An old standard from TV shows of yore.

How to Play

Instruct the group to sit on chairs in a circle.

One player stands in the middle, maybe the facilitator to start with.

The task for the players is to get the centre player to say 'Yes' or 'No' by asking questions.

Any kinds of questions are allowed.

Once 'Yes' or 'No' has been said, another player replaces the first.

Benefits of the Game

Attention, thinking skills, focus on a task, self-monitoring of speech.

Note

For many, the excitement lies in outwitting the centre player. It's not necessarily a fun task being in the centre; it can be something of an ordeal. So offering the chance of going in the centre to whomever 'gets the centre player out' may not work as a reward. Perhaps instead, that player can instruct someone else to go into the centre, as long as that person hasn't just come out.

ENGAGEMENT

Players	Age	Time
5+	10+	10

Numbers Game

Don't drift off, or you'll be at the bottom of the pile.

How to Play

Arrange a line of chairs facing the same way. Number each chair, 1, 2, 3 and so on from the end of the line. Ask the players to occupy the chairs. Clarify that the number refers to the *chair* not the *person*.

The person in chair number 1 is at the top of the line. His or her opposite number is at the bottom. The task for all the players is to get to the top of the line. Or, in the case of the player in chair number 1, to stay there.

This is achieved by not messing up as a focus is passed between the players. It goes like this: someone, e.g. the player in chair 8, stands up and says *'8 to 4'*. Now the player in chair 4 has to take and pass on the focus. This is done by standing and saying *'4 to 1'* (for example). The game continues until someone messes up. Messing up might involve getting words in a muddle, referring to a number that doesn't exist, giving one's own number wrongly, or standing too slowly.

When someone messes up, the game stops and that player goes to the bottom of the line, the farthest point from number 1. Everyone below that player's former position moves up a seat. The player who messed up is now in chair 8. Then the game resumes.

A time limit must eventually be given. Once the time is up, the player who is currently occupying chair number 1 is the winner.

Benefits of the Game

Attentiveness, focus, verbal communication.

Note

For players in wheelchairs, the instructions might be changed so that only a hand needs to be raised by the player who is passing the focus. Or the injunction to stand or raise an arm could be removed entirely.

Players	Age	Time
6+	10+	15

Numbers Game 2

Like poker only with fewer rules.

How to Play

Prepare some small pieces of paper, one for each member of the group. Write a number on each piece, starting with one and going up to the number of players.

One player should remain out of the game.

Ask the players to sit in a circle, holding their slips of paper, but not telling each other what the numbers are.

The remaining player stands in the centre of the circle. This player has to try and sit down.

He or she does this by calling out two numbers.

Players who have those two numbers have to swap places without the centre player getting one of those two seats.

Obviously the centre player doesn't know who has what number, so has to be alert to see who will move.

Other players also don't know who has what number, so a player called will have to try and secretly identify the other player to swap with.

If the players whose numbers have been called, manage to swap successfully, the centre player calls two new numbers.

The game continues until the centre player gets to sit down.

At this point the numbers are collected and redistributed.

Another game can then be played.

Benefits of the Game

Attentiveness, focus, reading body language.

+ Paper, pens		
Players	**Age**	**Time**
5+	10+	15

ENGAGEMENT

Hiss and Boo

It takes courage to be booed at.

How to Play

One player goes out of the room.

The other players define a task or series of tasks that the outside player needs to perform on return. Objects are placed in the space if necessary.

The outside player comes back in and has to work out what the required task is.

Indications of what the task is are communicated by the other players hissing or booing when the player is 'cold', i.e. doing actions that are away from the task, or 'hot', i.e. applauding when the player is getting close. The player needs to try stuff out to trigger these reactions.

When the task is accomplished, wild cheering is probably appropriate. Then another player goes out the room.

Benefits of the Game

Deductive reasoning, coping with failure, communication skills.

Note

Clues can always be given by the facilitator to prevent the player becoming too discouraged.

Players	Age	Time
6+	10+	15

Bang!

Having fun with killing and wounding.

How to Play

Players stand in a circle and are each given a number.

The facilitator calls out one number.

The player whose number it is has to duck as quickly as possible. Those on either side of that player have to 'shoot' that player before he or she ducks.

If the player ducks in time, the player on the other side of the ducking player may get shot instead.

One way or another, someone is going to be 'out'; either the one whose number is called because he or she was too slow to duck, or one of the other players because the called player ducked quickly and the other shooter shot fastest.

The player who loses leaves the circle.

The centre player calls out another number and the shooting begins again.

When there are only two players left, instruct them to stand back to back, and then count slowly to ten. At each count, the players take a step away from each other. Then leave out a number on the way to ten. As soon as the players hear a number missing, they have to turn and shoot each other.

Whoever shoots first is the overall winner.

Benefits of the Game

Speed of reaction, acceptance of failure, physical coordination.

Note

Strangely, this isn't the best game for young men with a history of firearm offences.

Players	Age	Time
8+	10+	15

Drama Nein Danke

'Drama? I ain't doin' that… are you mad!'

How to Play

Organise a circle of chairs and all sit down.

The facilitator sits in as well. He or she begins by pointing at someone. Explain that if a player is pointed at, they need to point at someone else immediately afterwards.

After a while of this, the players should add the phrase *'It was your fault'* when they point.

When it comes round again, players are asked to define what they are blaming the other player for. For example, *'It was your fault the party went wrong.'* And then to add a reason: *'Because you didn't buy any drink.'*

The player pointed at should then point at someone else and develop the story. *'It was your fault because you didn't give me any money for drink.'*

In this way a story, or backstory, is created.

Benefits of the Game

Converting a negative gesture into a creative piece of storytelling, teamwork, joining in a creative activity.

Variations and Extensions

It's open for the story to be developed further, perhaps through improvisation. Or for the story already created to be acted out.

Players	Age	Time
6+	12+	10

Ailments

Everyone likes to moan, especially in England.

How to Play

Instruct the players to walk around the room.

Then tell them that everyone has an 'ailment' which affects how they walk.

Tell them to invent a story that explains how they got the ailments. They should do this without talking to anyone else.

When everyone has an ailment and a story behind it, instruct the players to meet each other and exchange their stories.

It's all about having a moan.

However, when they separate, each player is instructed to take on the other player's ailment as well as his or her own.

So now each player has two ailments.

The players can then meet a second person.

Again, the story is the same, only this time each player tells two stories about two ailments, both of which are now their own.

Each player now walks away with four ailments.

Continue and the maths can get large.

Benefits of the Game

Interactiveness, storytelling, getting to know people in the group.

Variations and Extensions

I sometimes finish the game inside a doctor's surgery, playing the receptionist who has to go down the line finding out about the ailments before reporting to the doctor.

Players	Age	Time
8+	12+	15

Continuum

Find out about the group without asking personal questions.

How to Play

Ask the group to make a line with the tallest person at one end, the shortest at the other.

Ask the group to make a different line. Each new line is the answer to a different question.

Questions might be:

- '*What are people's shoe sizes?*'
    (with largest at one end, smallest at the other)
- '*What are people's birthdates?*'
    (with January 1st at one end)
- '*Who believes in God?*'
    (Strongly at one end, not at all at the other)
- '*Who believes in magic?*'
- '*Who believes popularity is important?*'

You can make up your own questions according to the character of the group.

Benefits of the Game

Learning about the group, generating discussion.

Variations and Extensions

The exercise works best as a springboard into conversation. From here you can always introduce topics such as themes for a show or a workshop. It can be used as a kind of fast-food focus group.

Players	Age	Time
6+	12+	15

Tin-Can Pulse

There are few better games to get back a group that's lost focus.

How to Play

Organise two teams of equal numbers. Each team sits on a line of chairs alongside each other, all facing the same direction. So in team 1, player A is in front of player B, and so on.

The task is for each team to accumulate points.

Points are won in one of two ways. First is by passing a message down the team fastest. The second is by the other team messing up and passing a message when it shouldn't be passed. A message must only be passed by touch, never sound.

The workshop leader sits at one end of the line. He or she tosses a coin in sight of the two players at the end, one from each team (only those two – all the rest must be looking the other way). If the coin comes up heads, it means a message should be passed. A tails means it shouldn't. The team that passes a message via touch to the end of its line first takes a point. At the far end of the line from the coin is a chair with a small object on it. On receipt of the message, each end player has to grab the object. The first to grab wins a point for that team (if the coin had been a heads).

However, if the coin is tails, and a message is sent incorrectly and the top player grabs the object, then the other team wins the point. If a team wins a point, all players in that team move up a seat. So the top player comes down to the bottom and everyone else moves up one.

The first team to five (or maybe ten) points is the winner.

Benefits of the Game

Focus, control of impulses, teamwork.

+ Small object, coin		
Players	**Age**	**Time**
8+	10+	15

ENGAGEMENT

ENGAGEMENT

Dog and Bone

Might have originated as a street game in the West Indies.

How to Play

Organise two teams who stand and face each other across a distance of at least fifteen feet, and place a short scarf between them on the floor.

Number off the players on both teams. Number 1 is opposite number 1, number 2 is opposite 2, and so on.

The task is for each team to accumulate points. This can be done in one of two ways: either by a player collecting the scarf and returning to their base position with it, without being touched by the opposite player. Or by touching the opposite player while he or she is carrying the scarf.

When all are ready, the facilitator calls out a random number. The two players who both have that number come forward and compete with each other.

Each tries to win the point, either by grabbing the scarf and running back, without being touched, or by waiting for the other to pick the scarf and trying to touch that player while he or she is carrying it.

The scarf can always be dropped by a player who wants to avoid being caught.

Rounds are played. The first team to a given number of points is the winning team.

Benefits of the Game

Energy, kinaesthetic skills.

Note

This can be a good game to get a reluctant group up and playing something. The lure of competition for some groups is hard to resist.

+ Scarf		
Players	**Age**	**Time**
8+	12+	15

The Don

This is a variation on 'The King Game'.

How to Play

Ask for a volunteer to play the part of a gang leader, who goes to the end of the room and sits down.

Secretly, agree with the Don a condition of entry into the gang. This should be something that can be demonstrated physically or verbally. It needs to be something that in the display is not easily spotted. For example, applicants to the gang have to have their hands in their pockets when they approach.

Then invite the rest of the group in turn to approach the Don with a view to gaining admission.

By approaching him or her, and succeeding or failing, they can learn what it is the Don requires. This involves some experimentation.

The Don sends back any player who fails the test.

He or she might give a clue. The others have to work out how to crack the code by watching.

As players crack the code, they are allowed to join the gang.

Players can have as many attempts as they like to join.

Benefits of the Game

The game employs subterfuge, so encourages skills of observation and deduction.

Note

Encouragement may be required for those players who fail to crack the code easily. When I worked with young offenders in Worcester, this is almost the only drama game they would agree to play.

Players	Age	Time
6+	14+	15

Working with Images

Photographs on a table always draw the eye.

How to Play

For this exercise, you need a good stock of same-size photographs or other pieces of visual art. A mix of realistic and abstract pieces works well.

Put all the images out on a table, ensuring there are at least three or four per member of the group.

Ask players to pick one picture each, any picture for any reason.

Invite each player to say why that picture was chosen.

Benefits of the Game

An introduction to story-making and discussion.

Variations and Extensions

Invite the group to work together to place the pictures in a sequence, in a way that tells a story. Ask for a volunteer to tell the whole story from beginning to end.

The group might also be divided into groups of two or three and each small group invited to make a story. More pictures could be made available. The story should be at least five pictures long. Then each small group can present to the larger, with one person acting as storyteller.

Note

I once ran this exercise with a group. One young man absolutely refused to pick a photograph. He said he thought they were '*all shit*'. So we asked him to pick the worst picture of all, the shittiest picture, the one he really couldn't stand. He picked a cartoon of a kid with a red face whose head was about to explode. And the thing was, the young man looked *exactly* like the kid in the picture…

+ Photographs		
Players	Age	Time
6+	14+	15

The Scarf Game

It's every woman for herself until there's only one standing...

How to Play

Give everyone in the group a short scarf, around two feet long.

All players have to tuck the scarf into the back of their trousers or skirt. The scarf needs to be clearly visible.

The aim is for each player to try and collect as many scarves as possible without having their own scarf taken.

On the word '*Go*', players move around freely trying to take other's scarves.

If a player loses his or her scarf, that player is out of the game, at least for that round. Scarves they have already collected can be retained but no further play is possible.

The winner is *either* the last player to lose a scarf *or* the player at the end of the game with the most stolen scarves.

Benefits of the Game

Physical awareness, kinaesthetic skills, observation, speed of movement.

+ Collection of scarves		
Players	**Age**	**Time**
8+	12+	10

ENGAGEMENT

Prisoner's Dilemma

Really a card game.

How to Play

Divide the group into two teams. If the total group size is over ten, this game is not appropriate – but you could get two games going simultaneously.

Each team has a set of cards (these need to be pre-prepared). The cards are as follows:

- A Cheat Card
- A Cooperate Card
- A Sit Tight Card
- A Joker Card

So each team holds four cards in total. In each round, teams play a card in the attempt to accumulate points. The art lies in second-guessing what the other team will play. Different combinations of cards accrue points differently:

- A Cheat card played against a Cooperate card, Cheat gets 6 points, Cooperate 1
- Cheat plays Cheat, both get 0 points
- Cooperate plays Cooperate, both get 6 points
- Cheat plays Sit Tight, Cheat gets 0, Sit Tight 2
- Sit Tight plays Cooperate, Sit Tight gets 2, Cooperate 4
- Sit Tight plays Sit Tight, they get 2 each

Each round involves the team playing one card against the other. The two cards have to be placed down simultaneously. The aim is for each team to accrue a winning number of points over a set number of rounds. It's all about tactics.

Benefits of the Game

Thoughtfulness, coping with failure, teamwork, learning the art of compromise.

+ Prepared cards		
Players	**Age**	**Time**
16+	14+	20

PART TWO

PLAY

These games and exercises rely less on robust mechanics and more on a voluntary commitment to imagination and spontaneity.

PLAY

No, You Didn't

The joys of contradicting your partner.

How to Play

Organise the group into pairs.

In each pair, player A tells a story, player B occasionally contradicts.

Player A begins their story. It can be purely invented or a real story.

Player B's occasional contradiction might be something like '*No, you didn't*' or '*No, she wasn't*' or '*No, it didn't happen like that*'.

On hearing the contradiction, the storyteller has to accept the denial and alter the story to fit the new information. The storyteller has, in other words, to accept the 'block' and refashion the story.

It's important that player B doesn't interrupt too often or the story will die.

After the story concludes or is concluded by the facilitator, the roles can switch.

Benefits of the Game

Acceptance, dealing with rejection of your ideas, learning to manage contradiction, flexibility of mind.

Note

If the storyteller opts to begin by telling a true story, they need to be able to deal with it being altered.

Players	Age	Time
4+	12+	10

Complete the Image

Developed out of an exercise from Augusto Boal, this game really has a much older feel to it.

How to Play

Organise the group to sit in a circle, either on chairs or on the floor.

One player comes into the circle and adopts a shape/strikes a pose.

Another player comes in and completes the image; in other words, joins the image, giving it a different or enhanced meaning. The two hold the image for a moment, and then the first player sits back down.

A third player jumps up and finds a different, frozen shape in response to the second player who has kept the same shape.

Then the second player sits down.

And so on.

Benefits of the Game

Observation, learning about complementarity, creative expression through images.

Variations and Extensions

A theme can be given as a starting point. This will tend to generate more literal images.

If they are comfortable with it, two players can do this exercise on their own as a physical dialogue. Here, each one responds to the last image of the other.

Or the two-person-image focus can become a three-person dialogue with two staying on each time and a third player adding to the image.

Or players can come in, find a physical shape and give a line of speech as they do so.

Players	Age	Time
10+	6+	15

PLAY

Antiques

Tends to appeal to the more opinionated and articulate group members.

How to Play

Organise the group into a circle, probably on chairs.

You need an object the nature and purpose of which is very ambiguous. It can be made of anything, but wood or metal objects are particularly effective.

The object is passed around the circle.

Everyone in the circle is an expert on antiques and can give an opinion on what the object is, where it comes from, what it's used for and its likely value.

No explanation is too absurd, providing a rationale is presented.

Each player is encouraged to disagree politely with the previous speaker and offer a completely different interpretation.

Everyone has to give a monetary value to the item.

Benefits of the Game

Articulacy, sharing of opinions with the group, the confirming of creative ideas.

+ Assorted objects		
Players	**Age**	**Time**
6+	12+	15

Changeable Object

A classic drama game whose gentle charms can still appeal.

How to Play

Organise the group to sit in a circle or in a line.

Place an object in the middle or in front of the group.

The object needs to be one with a simple shape or quality; a piece of cloth or wood is perfect.

The instruction is that you should pick up the object and endow it; in other words, you treat it 'as if' it was the object you have in mind. This will probably involve miming an action, using the object.

A wooden stick is treated as a sword.

A cloth is treated as a rag to a bull.

A frisbee is treated as a toilet lid.

Players are encouraged to come up one by one, and employ the object as if it was something different.

After a while, a different object can be placed in the middle, or possibly two objects.

Benefits of the Game

Use of imagination, flexibility of attitude, recognition of difference.

Variations and Extensions

Once one player has interacted with the object, another player can jump in to develop an improvisation with the first player, still keeping the object in focus.

+ Assorted objects		
Players	**Age**	**Time**
4+	12+	15

PLAY

Vampires

Not for those with a fear of being touched in the dark.

How to Play

Ask if there's anyone who is uncomfortable with keeping their eyes closed. If there is, these folk can sit out and watch, or act as 'guides'.

Explain the game.

It involves everyone being blindfolded and moving around the room at will.

The guides can ensure that players don't bump into walls or furniture.

Once blindfolds are on, the facilitator will give a tap to one of the players. This person will be a vampire. No one else will know who's been tapped.

The vampire's job is to create other vampires. This is done by either (the facilitator can decide on the rule) giving a shoulder tap to other players or by 'strangling' other players with the hands around the neck.

If a player is turned into a vampire, he or she needs to scream loudly.

That vampire then becomes able to create other new vampires.

If two vampires meet, they change each other back into ordinary humans. In which case they should moan with pleasure before resuming the game.

The game can run as long as it's working.

Benefits of the Game

Recreational mostly; engenders a sense of excitement and cultivates cooperation around rules.

Note

The game is best not played if the group is unable to accept the discipline of the rules.

+ Blindfolds		
Players	**Age**	**Time**
10+	12+	20

Shoes Game

Chaotic but, hopefully, managed chaos.

How to Play

Sit the group down in a circle.

Everyone takes off a shoe and holds it up in the air.

The facilitator needs to introduce a well-known tune or rhyming pattern which allows the game to be played.

Everyone sings the song.

At certain given words in the song – probably on the 'on' beat – players need to pass the shoe to their right and collect one from the left. The exercise is made more fun if on the other beats – the 'off' beats – the shoe is merely banged on the floor but not passed on.

The aim is to try and keep the game/song going without it all falling apart. If possible, up the tempo of the song as it goes on.

Benefits of the Game

Teamwork, sense of rhythm, playfulness, physical coordination.

Players	Age	Time
8+	10+	15

The Bears are Coming

There's nothing quite as pleasurable/frightening as the prospect of being eaten.

How to Play

Divide the group into bears and lumberjacks, with the large majority being lumberjacks.

The lumberjacks cut down trees in the Canadian redwood forest. However, there's a problem: the bears. The bears like to eat lumberjacks. However, if a bear can be fooled into thinking a lumberjack is merely a tree or a stone, then it will amble away.

The lumberjacks start cutting down trees and singing songs while the bears retire offstage. At a given cue, the bears will start growling. When this happens, the lumberjacks run around, shouting that the bears are coming. Then the bears are let in. At that moment, the lumberjacks go very still indeed.

The bears need to find out if these shapes are human. They can do this any way they like, but they can't use physical contact. Anything else is allowed. If the lumberjack/stone moves at all, it is 'eaten' immediately and becomes another bear.

After a short time, the bears are called offstage and the remaining lumberjacks go back to cutting trees. After a regroup, the bears are cued to start growling again. Then they reappear.

There should be several rounds of this. The 'winning' lumberjack is the last to be eaten.

Benefits of the Game

A sense of fun and playfulness, acceptance of simple rules, physical self-control.

Note

Clearly it's impossible to be completely, utterly still, so the facilitator might need to act as the referee, adjudicating on what is legitimate movement and what is clearly a loss of self-control.

Players	Age	Time
10+	12+	20

Cat and Mouse

This game works best with a larger number of young people.

How to Play

Organise the group into a grid but leave two players out. Everyone is standing. The grid looks something like this:

The two players left out are to play the roles of cat and mouse. The cat has to chase the mouse. If the cat catches the mouse, the mouse becomes the cat and the cat, the mouse. The territory of the chase is the grid.

However, if either the cat or mouse wants to drop out of the chase, he or she stands behind one of the other players. That other player immediately becomes that player's replacement – either the cat or the mouse.

Time can be called on the game when everyone's exhausted – or earlier.

Benefits of the Game

A sense of excitement and learning about rules engendering fair play.

Variations and Extensions

Additionally the players can join together to create corridors. This is done by putting up their arms so hands touch. The corridor can be made in either direction. The corridors created allow the chasing to take place within them. A clap or vocal signal from the facilitator can trigger everyone to swing round so that a new grid of corridors is created.

Players	Age	Time
12+	10+	15

Zoom – Screech

It's about waking everybody up.

How to Play

Organise the group into a circle.

Send a sound and movement around the circle one way. For example, 'zoom'. The gesture/sound zooms round the group.

Then introduce 'screech', which changes the direction of the zoom. So when a player has said screech, the zooms change direction.

Finally, you might introduce 'boing', which bounces the energy straight across the circle, is picked up by another player who zooms it around either way.

Penalties can always be introduced for messing up.

It's possible to characterise the game as a car zooming along, braking, reversing and being bounced back off a wall.

Benefits of the Game

Alertness, teamwork.

Players	Age	Time
6+	10+	10

Staring Competition

Antisocial behaviour turned to advantage.

How to Play

Set up a table with two chairs.

A player sits in either chair, other players are spectators.

The two players are each competing to out-stare the other.

The facilitator needs to act as referee.

As soon as someone blinks, that player is out and is replaced by a new player. The winning player stays on.

Benefits of the Game

Concentration, can involve members of the group who would otherwise avoid participating.

Players	Age	Time
4+	10+	10

PLAY

Word Smuggling
Just conversation with a twist.

How to Play

Divide the group into pairs.

Each pair sits down in their own area in the space.

Discreetly give one person in each pair a list of three words. The words should be in common usage but less common than 'and' or 'the'. Examples might be: 'carrot', 'envelope', 'army' or 'kidnap'.

The task for the player with the list is to smuggle the words into a conversation with the other player, without the other player identifying the key words.

The other player should have a pen and paper to write down the key words when he or she thinks they've been said. That player shouldn't let on their ideas during the conversation.

At the end of the conversation, the second player reads out what he or she thinks are the three smuggled words. A point can be counted for each one spotted.

Then the roles are reversed.

The second player is given a new set of three words.

A new conversation takes place.

The player with the winning points after so many rounds is the winner.

Benefits of the Game

Observation, communication skills, gets people talking.

+ Paper, pens, prepared words		
Players	**Age**	**Time**
4+	10+	10

Wizards, Giants, Elves

A game to use with a group that's full of cliques.

How to Play

Divide the group into two teams of equal number.

Each team is trying to wipe out the other team by capturing their members in a series of rounds.

In each round, each team plays as wizards, giants or elves.

The system is like 'Scissors, Stone, Paper'. Wizards beat giants because they put a spell on them. Giants beat elves because they can tread on them. Elves beat wizards because they can run up their cloaks and strangle them.

Teams decide who they are before the round begins. Everyone in the team plays the same role.

The ref counts '*One, two, three, four*'. On each beat, the teams advance on each other. On '*four*' they declare who they are by adopting the position – arms out front for wizards, crouching down for elves, standing tall for giants.

The team in a winning position can then 'capture' members of the other team by tagging them before they get back to their base.

If both teams have the same creature, there's muttering from both sides and no result.

Ensure that those captured accept to be part of the other team after capture, joining in the next round as part of that team.

The game continues until one team is wiped out, or the session runs out of time.

Benefits of the Game

Mixes up members of a large group.

Players	Age	Time
10+	10+	20

Russian Shoemakers

If you're going to use gibberish, then Russian gibberish is the best… the only problem I've had with this exercise was when there was a real Russian in the group.

How to Play

Explain to the group that every year in the Ural Mountains, shoemakers from all over the country come to celebrate their craft. The exercise starts with the moment when all the shoemakers arrive to greet their old friends – wearing their new, most contemporary shoes.

Everyone is pleased to see each other and they admire each other's shoes.

Everyone must greet each other in the grand style – in 'Russian', of course.

Once the rules are explained, everyone moves around the room, randomly greeting each other and showing off their shoes. Encourage players to be very expansive, to be proud of their shoes and, of course, to speak 'Russian' all the time.

After a while, it's possible to call a halt and move to the closing ceremony involving the mimed consumption of much alcohol and the many protestations of brotherhood and sisterhood.

Benefits of the Game

Physical contact, larger-than-life expressive behaviour, a certain abandon.

Players	Age	Time
10+	10+	10

The Egg Game

The meritocratic social system reduced to a game.

How to Play

Explain that there are three different roles to be played. The most junior is the egg. Next up is the bird. At the top of the ladder is the supreme being.

When you are an egg, you make an egg shape using your arms. When you are a bird, you flap your arms. When you are a supreme being, you move with your hands clasped as in prayer.

Everyone begins the game as an egg but aims to climb the evolutionary ladder.

Players are instructed to circulate around the space, just being an egg. If they want to challenge someone to a game that might allow them to move up the chain, they go up to another player and ask '*Would you like to play?*' If the challenge is accepted, both players face each other and put their hands behind their backs. They count to four together, and on four, bring their hands out front. Each must show their hands with a number of fingers pointing up. It's the first player to count the total number of fingers correctly who wins that round. The player who wins moves up one place so becomes a bird. The loser stays an egg.

If two birds then play each other, the winner becomes a supreme being and the loser goes back to being an egg.

Players can only challenge players who are on the same level as themselves. Eggs play eggs, birds birds, and so on.

The winner between two supreme beings stays at that level while the loser goes back to being a bird.

When the game ends, players at supreme being level are the winners.

Benefits of the Game

Dealing with failure, quickness of mind.

Players	Age	Time
10+	12+	20

PART THREE

COLLABORATION

These games and exercises get people working
together, using different means and different
degrees of cooperation.

Tug of War

A simple test to see how the group members are cooperating with each other.

How to Play

Divide the group into two teams.

Explain that you're going to stage a tug of war between the teams.

Only you've forgotten the rope.

So the tug of war will have to be staged as if the rope was really there.

It doesn't matter who wins, what's important is to see the tug of war played in such a way as it looks real with the two sides moving back and forth (but without the rope, of course).

Almost always, the desire to win will come to the surface and the two teams will instinctively move backwards – even though a 'win' proves nothing.

Usually the exercise has to be run two or three times before a convincing illusion is achieved.

Benefits of the Game

Teamwork, use of dramatic tension, physical skills.

+ Rope (kidding...)		
Players	**Age**	**Time**
8+	10+	10

On the Bus

Great for generating a sense of affirmation.

How to Play

Set up a bus. If you've only got chairs, that'll do.

The first player gets on the bus.

The second player comes on. This player should exhibit some kind of behaviour, e.g. singing a well-known song, talking on a mobile phone or being angry and kicking the chairs.

The first player has to immediately copy this new behaviour. So now there are two passengers talking on the phone or telling jokes to each other or waving to people outside the bus.

A third player gets on with a different mood or behaviour.

The first two need to adapt to the third.

The behaviour can be solitary which they each replicate, or it can involve dialogue.

Any number can get on the bus – the important thing is that as new players get on, all existing players copy them.

Players can also get off at any time and rejoin later.

Benefits of the Game

Generating a sense of acceptance, overcoming a sense of difference.

Note

The exercise can have a special resonance for groups whose members don't feel integrated into society or who have learning difficulties.

Players	Age	Time
8+	10+	15

COLLABORATION

Map of the Town

It's surprising how often drug users enjoy playing drug prevention officers.

How to Play

Divide everyone into groups of three or four before bringing everyone around a table.

Have on the table a large, hand-drawn map of an imaginary small town that you prepared earlier. The map will show the main street, shops, the cinema, library, police station, waste ground, a park, the estate, the rich areas, the poor areas, etc.

Ask the group where the drug-dealing would be likely to take place. Mark the group's suggestions on the map. It's likely there will be dealing in the nightclub and the park. There may be a crack den in the estate.

Then ask the group to switch their hats around and to think about dealing with the drug problem from the point of view of the local council. Ask them to take on roles of drug prevention officers.

Ask them to go into their groups and come up with strategies to tackle the drugs problem in the town. Ask them to think about positive alternative activities as well as punitive measures.

After twenty minutes or so, bring everyone back and get each group to present its proposals.

Finally, give some feedback to each of the groups – and get them to feedback to each other.

Benefits of the Game

Problem-solving, analysis, social perspectives.

Variations and Extensions

An alternative strategy would be to change the focus of the exercise. The question *'Where are the crime hotspots and what's going on there?'* will trigger a wider discussion on crime and crime prevention.

+ Paper, pens, a map of a town		
Players	**Age**	**Time**
6+	14+	30

Clint Eastwood

Based on the Eastwood principle of looking tough by instructing everyone else to look frightened.

How to Play

Ask the group to set up a café/bar area with tables and chairs.

Ask a volunteer to go outside the room, then to come back in as if he or she was visiting a café or bar. The volunteer should react honestly to what occurs, accepting the validity of the group's behaviour.

While the volunteer is outside, brief the remaining players. Explain that the exercise will be run several times with the volunteer coming in afresh each time. Explain that each time he or she comes in, the group will display a different reaction to his or her arrival.

- First time (for example): everyone stands, applauds and cheers.

- Second time: everyone stands and salutes.

- Third time: everyone goes quiet and starts whispering amongst themselves.

- Fourth time: everyone casts admiring glances.

- Fifth time: everyone hides under tables and chairs.

The point is for the volunteer to feel the force of the group's reactions and accept that there is justification for them.

The improvisation should in each case be played out with the volunteer going to the bar, ordering a drink, and trying to engage someone in conversation.

Feedback from the volunteer at the end of several 'runs' is important. How did he or she feel each time? What might have been the stories behind each version?

Benefits of the Game

Understanding how sensations, thoughts and emotions are triggered by the behaviour of others.

Players	Age	Time
8+	14+	15

Body Map

The kind of exercise you invent before realising that everyone else invented it years ago.

How to Play

You'll need extremely large pieces of white paper, big enough for someone to lie down on without touching the floor.

Divide the group into pairs.

In each pair, someone lies down on the paper while their partner draws a line in marker pen around the body. Then they change roles.

Participants take their pieces of paper, cutting the shape out, or leaving it in a frame.

The participant can then:

- Mark on details of particular incidents or accidents that are associated with those parts of the body.

- Attach cuttings from magazines that show aspirations for the future, again linked to parts of the body.

- Draw smaller figures within the larger figure showing growth from a baby, along with comments about what it was like to be that age.

Finally, participants bring their body maps back to the main group and talk about what they created. This discussion needs to be facilitated so that participants can be drawn out on their personal histories and aspirations.

Benefits of the Game

Sharing of histories, breaking down divisions.

Note

It's good to have a big selection of magazines that can be cut up as a resource to aid the process.

+ Paper, pens, magazines, scissors		
Players	**Age**	**Time**
4+	14+	30

The Identity Zone

Recognising that within one, there are many.

COLLABORATION

How to Play

Introduce the idea of every person being made up of many personalities. Ask participants about their different selves, especially how they show these differently to different people.

Ask everyone to create an 'identity zone' for themselves. This can be done alone or with a partner. For example:

- Cut images out of magazines in order to identify the different 'selves' that each participants has (instead of cut-out images, they could be drawn).

- Order these on a large, white piece of paper so that the 'self' that is shown most frequently is at the bottom/front of a vertical line of images.

- The 'self' that is shown hardly at all is at the back/top of the line.

Or you could start with this:

- Ask for a volunteer to define his or her different 'selves' and choose other players to represent these selves.

- The volunteer should give indication to each chosen player about how to represent that aspect of self, e.g. through a pose or gesture.

- Ask the volunteer to put his or her players in a line with the 'self' shown most frequently to the world, at the front and the 'hidden self' at the back.

- Ask the participant if there are changes he or she would like to make: *'What selves would you like to bring to the front?'*

Benefits of the Game

Self-analysis, self-development, sharing of personal information.

+ Paper, pens, magazines, scissors		
Players	**Age**	**Time**
4+	14+	30

The Truth About Drugs and Crime

A chance to come up with a film idea that beats what's currently in the cinemas.

How to Play

You'll need a large selection of strong photographic images. These should preferably be of dramatic, social interactions between people.

Divide everyone into groups; ask each group to pick several photos.

The task is to make up a storyline for a film, using these photos. A time limit should be set.

The exercise might usefully be preceded by a discussion about what makes a good film: character, plot, dilemmas, relationships, locations, story, etc.

Participants are encouraged to draw on their own experiences to devise a storyline. What's important is that the film should tell the audience 'the truth about drugs and crime' in some way or other. You might want to set the restriction of a '15' certificate.

Groups come back together and a volunteer outlines the idea for the story, using the photographs.

There's an option of a facilitator taking the role of a producer so this part of the exercise becomes a 'pitch session'. In which case, there needs to be a winner chosen, with reasons given for the choice.

Benefits of the Game

Use of imagination, learning about storytelling.

Note

This particular exercise was devised for young probation clients. For a different kind of group, a different subject area would be more appropriate.

+ Photographs		
Players	**Age**	**Time**
10+	16+	40

Hunting the Lion

'Follow My Leader', African-style.

How to Play

This works best for children or enthusiastic younger adults. (The book *Going on a Bear Hunt* is an acknowledged copy.)

Essentially it's a journey in which the leader leads the group through an African landscape in search of a lion.

The leader explains the mission to the group and urges everyone to follow him or her.

On the journey there is a thick jungle, a swampy river, heavy rain, holes in the ground, desert, dangerous animals, hunters, etc. On arriving at each new landscape, the leader instructs how to move across it or otherwise cope with the challenge. Heightened physicalisation is the norm, using, where possible, the spatial characteristics of the real environment: the room.

What happens when the lion is finally tracked down is up to you, but animal lovers will probably balk at anything less than a happy ending.

Benefits of the Game

Playfulness, physicality, a reckless spirit, a sense of connectedness between players.

Variations and Extensions

Depending on the ability of the players, extended improvisations can always be staged at different points in the journey.

Players	Age	Time
6+	4+	15

COLLABORATION

Newspaper Game

Lateral-thinking puzzles offer challenges that are very hard to resist.

How to Play

Take a broadsheet newspaper, separate the sheets and put a few pages down on the floor. Tell the group that everyone needs to be touching the newspaper and no one can be touching the floor, the walls or the furniture. Probably everyone will stand on the paper.

Reduce the amount of paper available. Same rules, you say. Second round. *'Everyone needs to be…'*, etc. Probably everyone will get on the paper again.

Paper is reduced again and as it's reduced, repeat the rules if necessary.

Soon the group will find it hard to squeeze on the paper. Don't alter the rules but scrupulously check there are no feet or other body parts on the floor. (Clothes and shoes are considered as parts of the body.)

Now the challenge for the group is to work out how to fulfil the rules, when standing on the paper doesn't work. They may tear up the paper and each stand on a small piece. They may attempt human pyramids.

There is only one way to fulfil the rules – which they will arrive at eventually. That is, each player holds a small piece of paper and jumps in the air.

Benefits of the Game

Lateral thinking, problem-solving.

Note

Questions for discussion: when did the task become difficult, and why? How was the breakthrough made? It is often difficult to change a strategy that has proved successful several times, but is now no longer working.

+ Sheets of newspaper		
Players	**Age**	**Time**
5+	14+	15

PART FOUR

SKILLS

These exercises are less game-like and more purposeful. Spontaneity gives way in part to thoughtfulness. The exercises aim to cultivate, nurture or test certain kinds of behaviours. In this way, they lend themselves more effectively to the enhancement of behavioural or social skills.

The chapter is broken down into sections, with each section listing exercises having different objectives. The first contains exercises that encourage *Observation* skills, the second is about *Reasoning* skills, the third is about *Kinaesthetic* (or physical) skills, the fourth deals with *Communication*, and the last is about the cultivation of *Performance* skills.

Observation

Kim's Game

I first played this in the Scouts with acorns, twigs and buttons.

How to Play

Organise a tray or table of very small objects, about twenty in number; probably an assortment of the mundane and peculiar is best: a pencil, a stamp, a coin, a plastic finger with blood…

Cover with a cloth.

Organise the group into pairs.

Explain that everyone will have about a minute to observe the objects. The aim is to memorise as many as possible.

Lift the cloth and show the objects for one minute.

Give each pair a pencil and paper.

The task is for each pair to write down as many objects as they can remember.

Collect the papers after two minutes.

The pair who remembered the most objects correctly is the winner.

Benefits of the Game

Observation, memory, teamwork.

Variations and Extensions

It is possible to run other activities after observation of the objects but before recording them. For example, after the pairs have looked at the objects, the facilitator might run a discussion about something completely unconnected or organise a physical game. Only after this do the pairs get to sit down and write their lists.

+ Assorted small objects		
Players	**Age**	**Time**
4+	6+	15

The Behaviour of the Room

Developed out of an exercise used by Augusto Boal called 'Change Three Things'.

How to Play

Ask for a volunteer.

The volunteer needs to stand at one end of the room.

Everyone else takes a position in the room, the poses can be as mad as they like.

The volunteer acts as an observer and looks closely at how everyone is sitting or standing, what they are wearing and at the objects in the room. There's up to a minute for this.

Then the observer turns to face the wall.

Three changes are then made to the room, its objects or its occupants. A chair is moved, someone changes position and perhaps a picture's position is altered.

The observer turns back and has to identify as many of the three changes as possible.

The exercise can then be repeated with another player. As the game progresses and players get used to the rules, the changes can get more and more subtle to really test their observation and concentration skills.

Benefits of the Game

Observation, patience, memory.

Players	Age	Time
4+	12+	10

Find Your Gang

There's someone out there who can give you that sense of belonging.

How to Play

The exercise works best if the group numbers twelve or more.

Have a piece of paper for each player and group the pieces into three sets. On all the pieces in one set write down a kind of behaviour, for example, 'Walk slowly and keep looking behind you'. Then for another set, 'Walk slowly and look at the ground', and the third, 'Walk with your hands in your pockets'.

Each set of papers also has a keyword attached to it. 'Walk slowly and keep looking behind you' might have the word 'Blue', for example. Other sets will have other, different words, like 'Apple' or 'Loud'.

Distribute all the pieces of paper and tell the players to conceal the content.

Each player is now part of a three-person gang, but they don't know who the other gang members are.

Organise an activity, for example, tidying up the room or playing a different theatre game, during which the players must subtly display their behaviour while observing the others.

During the activity or game, players can approach each other to find out if they are in the same gang. The aim is not to ask directly but instead use the keyword and to see if it's recognised.

The game ends when all the gangs have been created.

If played competitively, then it's a case of which gang meets first.

Benefits of the Game

Observation, kinaesthetic skills, communication skills.

+ Paper, pens		
Players	**Age**	**Time**
12+	8+	10

The Big Picture

The bigger the better.

How to Play

You need a large photographic image, perhaps reproduced in a newspaper. Failing that a drawing or painting, but an abstract image won't work so well.

This exercise can be run as all-against-all or pairs competing with each other.

Ask for a volunteer or maybe two.

The volunteer/s have one minute to examine the picture. It's then removed from sight and given to the rest of the group.

The rest of the group ask the player/s five questions about the picture: '*What colour is the woman's hat?*' '*How many bananas are there?*' The questions need to be moderated, i.e. checked by the facilitator so that they aren't too hard.

The exercise is then repeated with a different picture and a different competitor – or two.

The player/s with the most correct answers are the winners.

Benefits of the Game

Observation, memory recall, attention to detail.

Variations and Extensions

The exercise might be played with the facilitator showing the picture to all the players and asking everyone the questions. All the players then write down their answers and the player with the most correct answers is the winner.

+ Large photographic images		
Players	**Age**	**Time**
6+	8+	10

Bandleader

Perspective is all.

How to Play

Organise the group to sit in a circle on the floor or on chairs and ask for a volunteer.

Explain that this is a copying game where the copying needs to be discreet. The aim for the group is to copy the 'bandleader' – who will be sitting somewhere round the circle – without the volunteer in the middle discovering who it is.

Send the volunteer out of the room if possible.

Nominate – or invite someone to self-nominate – to be the bandleader. Get that person moving, clapping or gesturing, possibly on a rhythm, and invite the volunteer back into the room.

The volunteer should sit in the middle of the circle.

Now the bandleader should subtly start changing the rhythm or character of the sound/movement. The others should follow.

The task for the observer is to identify the bandleader as early as possible. Best of all is with the first guess.

The copying needs to be subtle otherwise the observer will identify the bandleader too quickly.

Perhaps four other guesses are available to the observer, depending on the size of the group.

The exercise is ended either with the correct guess or by the observer running out of guesses.

Another player can be invited to be the observer – perhaps the former bandleader.

Benefits of the Game

Observation, group cohesion, kinaesthetic skills.

Players	Age	Time
6+	**6+**	**10**

Whose Story is True?

Especially for liars and those who can spot them.

How to Play

Divide everyone into groups of four or five.

Explain that in each group, every member should tell a true story to the others in their group. This should be done quietly so other groups don't hear the stories. The story should be from childhood and should involve mischief or an accident. It should not involve death or tragedy.

Once the stories have been told, each group needs to select one for the exercise.

In the exercise, all the players in that group are going to learn that story as if it was their own. And be ready to tell it.

Allow some time for this. Then everyone comes back together.

One group sits in front of the rest and each person tells the same story. '*I was fourteen and I stole a car...*' Everyone gives more or less the same account. But of course only one person is telling their own true story. The aim is to misdirect the audience as to who the genuine storyteller is. The aim for the audience is to work out who is telling the truth.

The spectators may then question the storytellers about their accounts. Probably no more than one question per spectator is useful.

Finally, each spectator needs to make a decision about who is telling the truth. Can the liars be spotted? What is the body language of the tellers indicating?

A group of successful tellers will have duped everyone.

Benefits of the Game

Observation, awareness of body language, storytelling, working with an audience.

Players	Age	Time
6+	12+	30

Reasoning

SKILLS – Reasoning

Predicaments

For those groups who are mature enough to process information through physical touch.

How to Play

Explain that the exercise involves blindfolds and this is the chance to opt out if anyone feels uncomfortable moving without sight.

Divide everyone into two groups of equal number. One group needs to put on blindfolds.

Then the other group puts each member of the blindfolded group into a physical position that represents a scene.

For example, they are all individuals involved in a traffic accident: there's a wounded bicyclist, a policeman, a passer-by, a member of the public, etc.

It works well if each member of the sighted group takes responsibility for 'sculpting' a different member of the blindfolded group.

Once in position, the blindfolded players need to talk to each other and describe their positions.

Then they have to work out what each player within the scene is doing and what kind of incident or scene is occurring. Encourage them to be quite analytical and descriptive at first, and only after this to start the guesswork. The sighted group shouldn't interfere.

Once the correct conclusion is arrived at, the groups swap over.

Benefits of the Game

Communication, deductive reasoning, coping with inadequate information, kinaesthetic skills.

Variations and Extensions

This is the reverse of game 63: *Shapes in the Dark* (page 74).

+ Blindfolds		
Players	**Age**	**Time**
6+	18+	20

Press-Ups

On the surface this would seem to be about physical skills but it's really a problem-solving task.

How to Play

Explain to the group that it needs to work on a problem and solve it together.

The task is: everyone must do a press-up at the same time but without anyone's feet touching the floor.

No furniture or walls can be used to solve the problem.

The answer lies in creating a circle with everyone's feet on everyone else's back.

But obviously you don't tell them that.

Benefits of the Game

Problem-solving, collaboration, a sense of achievement on completion.

Players	Age	Time
8+	12+	10

Shortest Time Possible

A lateral-thinking puzzle that shifts participants away from obvious solutions.

How to Play

You need balls for this one.

Ask the group to stand in a circle.

Throw a ball to one person across the circle then ask that person to throw it to someone else and for that person... etc. until everyone has received and passed the ball once only.

Ask people to remember the journey of the ball.

Send the ball on the same journey a few times.

Then after sending the ball, send a second ball, then a third.

Depending on the size of the group, send round about six or eight balls.

Then tell the group to see how quickly it can get all balls round that journey from the moment the first one goes to the moment the last one comes back.

Time how long it takes. Then ask how the time might be reduced.

Initially, suggestions will focus on throwing and catching more efficiently.

Get the time down this way.

Then ask for more creative suggestions to get the time down.

Explain that what's important is that the balls must all 'pass through the hands of each player in the correct order'.

The fastest way of all will probably be for all the balls to be dropped through a series of hands held – in the correct order – vertically, creating a tunnel.

Benefits of the Game

Problem-solving, teamwork.

+ Juggling balls		
Players	**Age**	**Time**
6+	12+	10

Name That Object

In which the impatient will fall to arguing amongst themselves.

How to Play

Ask for three volunteers.

You need a modest collection of small objects: a hairbrush, a cotton reel, a dead fly…

Place one of the objects out of sight of the three volunteers but in sight of the rest of the group. The easiest way to achieve this is by placing the item on a high-backed chair that faces away from the three volunteers.

Have everyone sit down, ensuring the object remains masked from the three.

The task for the three is to work out what the object is. The only way they can do this is by asking questions of the rest of the group; questions to which the answer can only be either yes or no. The aim is to find the solution in as few questions as possible.

They will very likely start with questions like *'Is there a limit to the number of questions we can have?'* and *'Does it matter who asks the question?'* and possibly *'Can we ask any kind of question?'* Given that the answers to these questions are 'No', 'No' and 'Yes', that'll be three questions gone already.

Once this group of three have successfully identified the object, another three take their place and a different object is selected.

The team with the fewest number of questions before getting to the right answer is the winner.

Benefits of the Game

Thinking skills, cooperation, mental self-discipline.

+ Assorted small objects		
Players	**Age**	**Time**
6+	14+	15

Obstacle Race

Not really obstacles and not really a race.

How to Play

Take a table, a chair and a book.

Put them in a line across the floor of the room.

Send half of the group out of the room.

With the other half, work out an imagined route through/over/by these objects.

For example, the route is crawl under the table, climb over the chair and walk round the book. This would be the obvious route but you could mix it up: '*Go over the table, sit on the chair and jump over the book.*'

This is the journey that the outside group have to discover.

Invite them back in and explain that there is a journey through/over/by these objects.

They have twenty questions in which to discover the route. The questions have to invite '*Yes*' or '*No*' answers only.

Once the code has been cracked and congratulations offered, ask the next group to step out, rearrange the objects and devise a new journey.

The team that cracks the code of their journey in the smallest number of questions is the winner.

Benefits of the Game

Teamwork, deductive reasoning, patience, learning not to hate the other team who set such an impossible task.

Variations and Extensions

You might substitute the table, chair and book for other objects.

+ Table, chair, book		
Players	**Age**	**Time**
6+	14+	20

Missing Character

Like those dreams where you know you should be doing something really important straight away, but you can't for the life of you think what it is.

How to Play

Ask for a volunteer to go outside the room.

With the rest of the group, invent a situation where people are engaged in activity. It could be a scene of conflict or collaboration; a fight or putting up a tent. But the point is that within this scene is a role that must be discovered by the other player. If it's after a fight, it might be that of the person who caused the fight. If putting up a tent, it might be the person who holds the mid-section pole.

Invite the volunteer into the room. He or she has to work out what the missing role is and then play it. The players improvise the scene so the volunteer can watch, but they improvise as if they were waiting for the missing character to turn up. So if it's the fight story, it might be young people doing some kind of punishment after the fight. If it's the tent, there's wrestling with the tent, and failing.

If the volunteer makes a guess and it's wrong, the players keep playing the scene. If correct, then the volunteer joins in the scene and it continues as an improvisation with all involved.

Benefits of the Game

Deductive reasoning, coping with lack of information, coping with being the outsider.

Note

One of the best interpretations I saw of this challenge was a group of young prison inmates who decided they were a Formula One pit-stop team that changed tyres on the cars. When the volunteer stood precisely where the racing driver would be, they spun into action, changing tyres in a rush and jumping away.

Players	Age	Time
6+	12+	20

What Happened Here?

About discovering the backstory.

How to Play

This exercise requires a little setting up.

The group needs to leave the space, supervised if necessary.

The performers or facilitators invent a story based around an event that's taken place. Within the space, they set up a scene which shows the aftermath of the event. Furniture or props are used.

Then the performers place themselves as characters in that situation.

Examples of situations might include: a father has injured his son in an argument about the son going off to fight in a war. Or someone has visited a friend expecting they will go on holiday together but the friend has refused to go.

The group is let back in. The group's task is to work out who these characters are and what just happened.

The group members can ask questions of the characters.

The actors must answer in character while avoiding giving the game away too easily.

The exercise should be run with a view to a discussion after it, looking at the issues raised by the piece.

Benefits of the Game

Analytical reasoning, understanding relationships, looking below the surface.

Note

The more there is to discover, the more interesting and engaging the journey of discovery.

+ Assorted props		
Players	**Age**	**Time**
4+	14+	30

Priorities

On leaving prison.

How to Play

Explain to a volunteer that this is about setting priorities on your first day out of jail. There are people competing for your attention and you have to decide a plan for the day. Let's call this character Joe. Then ask Joe to leave the room.

Everyone remaining will be given a role. A set of pre-printed cards with the roles on could be handed out, or the descriptions given verbally. Each role is a character in Joe's life (examples here are for a male group):

- A probation officer who needs to see Joe at 2 p.m.

- His father who expects him to come straight home and spend the rest of the day there.

- His mate John who is waiting at the gate and is expecting to go on a pub crawl for the day.

- Terry, a football coach who is expecting to see Joe on his first day out.

- Pete who has been promised some money when Joe gets out, money owed since he went inside.

- Mohammed who is waiting at his mother's house and needs Joe to sign up for a charity walk.

Joe comes back in and hears what all the characters have to say to him. He then has a few minutes to prepare his plan for the day.

He returns to the group to explain his plans. The group members respond in role to his suggestions. He listens to them and, at that point, may or may not change his priorities.

Finally, all participants come out of role and the decisions of Joe become subject to discussion.

Benefits of the Game

Problem-solving, managing relationships, time management.

Players	Age	Time
6+	16+	30

SKILLS – Reasoning

The Balloon

What goes up…

How to Play

Ask the group to sit closely together on chairs.

Allocate professional roles to each: doctor, teacher, artist, plumber, lorry driver, farmer, etc. Ensure the roles are very different.

Explain that everyone is in a hot-air balloon floating in the sky.

But the balloon is losing height and may crash into the sea, so there's a danger everyone will drown before the destination is reached.

However, if someone can be sacrificed, they might reach their destination.

Whoever is thrown out of the balloon may survive but may not.

Each player has to argue a case on their own behalf to stay in the balloon – or argue on behalf of someone else to stay in. The question to debate is '*Who is most valuable to society – and why?*'

Finally, a vote is taken on each character in the balloon. Whichever character receives the fewest votes has to jump. If there are two with the same small number of votes, then they each make a pitch for themselves and the rest of the group votes between them. (You are not allowed to vote for yourself.)

After one role/player has been sacrificed, the same procedure can be imposed again.

The exercise ends when there's only one player left.

Benefits of the Game

Holistic thinking, communication skills, social analysis.

Players	Age	Time
6+	14+	30

Gossip

When truth ends and lies begin, the line is hard to find.

How to Play

Several of the group are cast as gossips.

Another player is cast as a character called, for example, Zoe.

A scene is set up in which the gossips moan and bitch about another character, let's call this character Jane. (It's important that the role of Jane has not been cast. It's also important to establish that all the allegations made against Jane are groundless and fictional.)

In this scene, Zoe overhears what is said about Jane.

The role of Jane is now cast from someone else in the group.

Zoe then has to explain to Jane what was said in the gossip and the two have to decide on a course of action.

Whatever they come up with by way of strategy should be tried out as a role play or improvisation. Other players can be cast in other roles, such as teachers or parents.

For example, she wants to confront the group directly. Or she wants to speak to one member of the group separately. Or she wants to go to a parent or teacher for advice.

The sequence of improvisations can continue as long as it's useful.

Benefits of the Game

Dealing with conflict and anxiety, communication and negotiation skills, problem-solving.

Players	Age	Time
6+	12+	20

Kinaesthetic

Boxing

Only for those who know the difference between playing and fighting.

How to Play

Divide the group into pairs. It may be an advantage if this is done on the basis of height. Gender isn't significant here, although girls may feel more comfortable working together.

Explain that each player is going to have a boxing match with his or her partner. All the rules of boxing are applied – only in reverse:

- Players mustn't have any physical contact at all but should react *as if* there was contact.
- Players box in slow motion rather than real time.
- Players don't try to win but rather 'create a match with that player' in which either player may win.

For young men particularly, this can be a bit of a headfuck. They will find it hard to curb the instinct to win, so observe carefully to ensure the rules are followed. The emphasis should be on play and theatricalisation. Encourage a view that losing is more fun than winning. Everyone should understand this is a performance of a boxing match, not a real boxing match.

Switch partners as necessary.

You can always end the exercise with a free for all in a Wild West saloon. At the end, there's only one player standing.

Benefits of the Game

Kinaesthetic skills, observation, cooperation, learning about weight, sensation and physical balance.

Note

In this exercise, which I learned from Augusto Boal, physical strength and gender difference are of no significance.

Players	Age	Time
8+	12+	10

Sticks

A very clear opportunity for misuse of the tools, so be confident the group won't be tempted.

How to Play

Bring enough sticks for the whole group, one each.

Sticks should be around three to four foot long, lightweight but not so flimsy that they won't carry cleanly in the air.

Divide the group into pairs. Each pair should practise throwing the sticks to each other.

The stick is thrown from its centre so in the air it's perpendicular or clearly pointed upwards. It shouldn't be thrown like a javelin. (If there's any danger of that happening, don't play this game, there are plenty of weapon-free exercises…) It should be caught with one hand only.

Initially, the pair practises with just one stick between them. It's important always to get eye contact with the other player before throwing.

Then they move on to throwing two sticks between them and catching two sticks simultaneously.

When all the pairs have mastered this, the group walk about the room. The aim now is for each player to catch someone's eye while walking and when this is achieved, for these two players to throw the sticks between them.

When the group is walking, throwing and catching without too much difficulty, the pace of walking can be increased. The group can now run or jog gently around the room, throwing and catching sticks. As long as the rule about the sticks being thrown vertically is upheld, there should be no problem.

Inevitably some sticks will fall to the ground.

Benefits of the Game

Physical coordination, balance, teamwork.

+ Bamboo or wooden sticks		
Players	**Age**	**Time**
6+	14+	15

Shapes in the Dark

Involves a degree of physical contact.

How to Play

Organise everyone so you have two groups of three or four players each. Others can watch until the exercise repeats.

There needs to be the same number of people in each of these two groups. (It's useful if each player has a buddy in the other group.)

One group closes its eyes. Blindfolds may be useful here because the group has to stay 'blind' for several minutes.

A second group takes up positions together to make a collective image of some kind. The image can be purely abstract.

It's good if these players are quite close to each other or have some physical contact. They need to hold that still image for several minutes.

The first, blindfolded group then have to go and make contact with the other group, using their hands, and from the information gained without sight, work out what the body shapes are.

This group should try and make either a mirror (reversed) or an exact copy of that image. If a buddy system has been used, each player touches and copies a buddy.

When the blindfolded group have done their best, they open their eyes or remove blindfolds, while still in position. They can then see how far they've replicated the image.

The exercise can be run again with the two groups reversing or with two new groups.

Benefits of the Game

Kinaesthetic skills, familiarity with physical contact, imaging skills.

+ Blindfolds (optional)		
Players	**Age**	**Time**
6+	16+	20

SKILLS – Kinaesthetic

Journeys

Into imagination…

How to Play

Divide the group into pairs.

Give each pair a blindfold, and ask for one in each pair to be blindfolded.

The sighted player will lead the blindfolded player around the room. This is best done by one player taking the hand of the blindfolded player and putting his or her hand in touch with objects. The aim is to create a number of sensory experiences for the blindfolded player, through physical objects, walls and furniture.

Initially, discourage physical contact between blindfolded players.

Ensure that safety of the blindfolded players is maintained at all times.

Encourage a discussion of the journeys once completed, either within the pairs or within the whole group.

Benefits of the Game

Trust, heightened sensory contact, imagination.

Variations and Extensions

The sighted player takes the blindfolded player on an imaginative journey rather than a literal one. They both travel together through a dangerous terrain. There's crawling through tunnels, wading through water and dodging behind walls. All is created by the words of the sighted player, encouraging and exhorting the other. What's important is that the journey is undertaken by both together; both are rained on, both get wet, both are shot at, both get shot.

+ Blindfolds		
Players	**Age**	**Time**
6+	14+	20

Fast-Food Martial Arts

A quick way to find out who has good physical coordination and balance skills.

How to Play

Get two players to stand facing each other, with a yard or so between them.

Each stands with feet slightly apart.

Both players put out their hands towards the other. The players should be able to touch each other's palms easily.

The aim of the exercise is to cause the other player to move his or her feet. The only physical contact allowed is palm to palm. The aim might be achieved by pushing against the other's hands to knock them off balance, or sharply moving one's own hands back, to the same end.

It can be run as a points game or, alternatively, the winner always 'stays on'.

Benefits of the Game

Balance, physical coordination, kinaesthetic skills.

Note

It can be a good move to demonstrate the exercise by being one of the first two players. In which case it runs as a challenge exercise in which the challenge is thrown out to all comers.

(My editor has suggested this might be run using blindfolds – I haven't tried that and I suspect he hasn't. Sounds promising but you might want to try it with crash helmets first.)

Players	Age	Time
4+	12+	10

Lightest Point of Contact

So you're barely touching.

How to Play

Divide the group into pairs.

Each pair has to find a point of contact with the other player which is the lightest possible contact.

This is probably going to be by fingers.

This can be done with both players sighted or with one player blindfolded.

One player leads the other about the room.

After a while, give a command, *'Change'*, and then the other player has to start leading.

After another while, give another *'Change'* command and now the pair have to move around the room with neither leading but both staying in light physical contact.

Benefits of the Game

Sensitivity, coordination, teamwork.

Variations and Extensions

It's possible to specify points of physical contact, e.g. backs, shoulders, legs, etc. Music can also be added to enable the group to turn the exercise into something closer to contact improvisation or dance.

The light physical contact rule can also be relaxed so it becomes a more intense contact.

+ Blindfolds, recorded music		
Players	**Age**	**Time**
6+	10+	10

Communication

The Argument Game

You need to be prepared to argue against yourself.

How to Play

Ask three members of the group to sit down in a line all facing the same way.

The rest of the group sits opposite them, making an audience.

Two of the players in the line of three are going to debate with each other on a given topic while between them sits a referee. It's best if the referee sits slightly behind the other two.

A topic is given to the players. It needs to be a topic that the group is happy to argue about.

For example, player A is going to argue in favour of the legalisation of drugs while player C is going to argue against. Player B is the ref.

The debate begins.

Every so often the referee is going to tap one player or the other on the shoulder. When that player is touched, the player has to reverse his or her position within the argument. If the ref touches player A, that player has to immediately argue *against* the legalisation of drugs. So at this point, the two players are agreeing with each other. Until the referee makes another touch.

Benefits of the Game

The benefits lie in increased articulacy, mental flexibility and the ability to argue a case. But it's a hard exercise.

Note

It's important the referee doesn't change the polarities of the debate too often or the players just become confused. It may be best if the facilitator acts as the referee, at least initially.

Players	Age	Time
6+	14+	10

I'm a Celebrity Prisoner, Get Me Out of Here!

This is a game that makes most sense for those in custodial settings.

How to Play

Divide the group into pairs. Explain that this exercise is about arguing on behalf of someone else, not yourself. The government has decided that due to prison overcrowding, a limited number of prisoners will be released early. Each player has to advance the case for his or her partner to be on that list.

So if Joe and Ali are working together, Joe makes the case for Ali to be released, and vice versa. Therefore Joe has to brief Ali extensively, and Ali, Joe. It's important that the participants understand this is about *real* lives and *real* personal stories. So information about the candidate's plans for release, family responsibilities and dreams for the future is all relevant.

When all the players are ready, they are brought before an Early Release Board, perhaps consisting of one facilitator and one player who hasn't participated in the exercise. Each player then makes the case for his or her partner.

Then a decision is made by the panel. The reasons why that individual has been chosen need to be given.

Benefits of the Game

Reasoning skills, managing argument.

Variations and Extensions

Instead of being released from prison, the government is making available £5,000 grants to individuals experiencing hardship or who have a powerful need for finance. The grant can be used directly for that individual, or towards a cause of their choosing. Only one grant can be awarded.

Players	Age	Time
6+	16+	30

Word Smuggling 2

Calls for essential skills such as deception, misdirection and the use of a poker face.

How to Play

Divide the group into pairs.

You'll need a list of slightly unusual words, or even better, several short lists of around four words each.

Good words would be 'autocrat', 'diner', 'tomato', 'carpet', 'geriatric', 'elephant', 'collapse' or 'environment'. Too difficult words would be 'psoriasis', 'gerund', 'tautology' or 'dynastic'. Too easy words would be 'and', 'now', 'get', 'out', 'of', 'here'.

Explain to the pairs that each pair will have a conversation. It can be about anything at all. However, one player in each pair must try and smuggle words from his or her list into the conversation.

Give the smuggler in each pair a list of around four words.

Tell the other players not to interrupt during the conversation, but simply to remember or note down words suspected of being smuggled words.

After five minutes of chat, call time out and ask the second player in each pair what words they've spotted – are these the correct words?

Switch roles and give out new lists.

Benefits of the Game

Attentiveness, use of vocabulary, communication skills.

+ Paper, pens, prepared words		
Players	**Age**	**Time**
4+	12+	10

Animals / Drink / Sport

The old game of 'Charades' kicked around a little.

How to Play

Divide the group into teams of around four players each.

Preferably there will be two or four teams.

Ask each team to create a list of words under several categories:

- Animal
- Drink
- Sport
- Job or profession
- Hobby
- Film title

Team A then gives its list discreetly to one member of team B. This team B member has to communicate each item on the list to his or her team members without using words. The team has the generic list in front of them: animal, drink, etc., so they know the first item will be an animal, the second a drink, etc.

The exercise is best played with the communicator standing up and the facilitator acting as referee.

It's a competition against the clock. The team that communicates the list in the shortest time is the winner.

If there are four teams, then team C can play team D as a second semi-final with a final play-off between the two successful teams.

Benefits of the Game

Non-verbal communication, coping with pressure.

+ Paper, pens		
Players	**Age**	**Time**
6+	12+	30

Minefield

When blind and sighted worlds attempt to collaborate.

How to Play

Fill the room with furniture (tables, chairs) and large props (stuffed animals if you have them, or anything available). Ensure these items are spread consistently and evenly throughout the space.

Divide the group into pairs. Explain that this is about communication between a sighted and a blind partner across a minefield. One partner in each pair will wear a blindfold; the other is a guide.

The sighted player directs their partner across the space, using verbal instruction, without the blindfolded player touching any of the 'mines'. The sighted player therefore remains at the start point, one end of the room, directing the other to the finish point at the far end.

The aim is for the blindfolded player to get across in as short a time as possible, while avoiding mines. If a mine is touched, then thirty seconds (for example) will be added to the time of this pair.

First one pair goes; then the next pair goes. The timing for each pair is recorded. When all the pairs have gone, they should go again with the players within pairs switching roles.

Once all the pairs have gone twice, each pair will have two recorded times. These can be added together to give a total time for each pair. The pair with the shortest overall time is the winner.

Benefits of the Game

Verbal communication skills, patience.

Note

It's useful to periodically move the furniture in the space so the route can't be memorised.

+ Blindfolds, tables, chairs, stuffed animal, etc.		
Players	**Age**	**Time**
6+	12+	20

Chinese Mime

Like the 'Whispers', only without words.

How to Play

Divide the group into teams of about six players each. If there are only six, simply play with one team.

Send all players out of the room, apart from one. Give that player a story, it could be handed over as text or told verbally. The story should have one central character who does various things and to whom things happen. For example, a man wakes up in the morning, goes outdoors, has his foot run over by a bus... Or a bad Queen is admiring herself in the mirror when she finds an enormous spot... The story should have a beginning, middle and end.

Everyone comes back in. The player now has to act out the story to another person in his or her team without using words. The rest of the team face the wall. The rest of the group watch as an audience.

When this is done, the player who has just watched the mime, acts it out for the next team member. And so on. (It's important the players never see the story enacted until it's their turn to watch.) In this way, the story is passed along like 'Chinese Whispers'.

Finally, the last member in the team tells everyone what he or she thinks the story is.

Then the process repeats for the other team with a different story.

Benefits of the Game

Non-verbal communication, storytelling, memory.

Note

What's interesting to note in feedback is which narrative elements were retained, and which were lost. We all try to make sense of material placed in front of us, and tend to fill in gaps to compensate for information deficits. If the guesses are wrong, an entire story can become tilted in the wrong direction.

Players	Age	Time
6+	14+	30

The Argument Room

Don't go in there in a bad mood.

How to Play

Set up a rectangle of chairs delineating the Argument Room.

Explain that the exercise is about carrying out a task without getting into an argument. A player needs to enter the Argument Room and sit down. He or she becomes the occupant.

The task is for a visitor to go into the room and give the occupant some information. This needs to be prepared in advance by the visitor. For example, the visitor has to tell something about him or herself: likes, dislikes, interests, etc., almost as a profile that you would create on Facebook. The occupant of the room has to write this information down but while doing so, try and get the visitor into an argument. This can be done discreetly, blatantly or outrageously. Use of contradiction is encouraged. Personal insults are not permitted, and breaking of this rule should result in extreme punishment or, given the inadvisability of torture on health and safety grounds, banishment from the room.

Can the visitor resist being drawn into an argument? That's the challenge. Every time the visitor gets into an argument, he or she has to leave the room. The facilitator is the referee. If the visitor lasts three or five minutes, for example, points or prizes can be achieved.

Change occupants and visitors periodically.

Benefits of the Game

Self-control, negotiation skills.

Note

The task of the visitor might alternatively be practical; for example, it involves cleaning the space or building something in there.

+ Paper, pens, chairs, watch		
Players	**Age**	**Time**
6+	12+	30

Community Centre

Some things are just nobody's fault (apparently).

How to Play

Ask everyone to sit on chairs in a circle.

Explain that everyone in the group will play a role of someone who is connected to a community centre in the local town or city.

There has been an incident where the centre's windows were broken.

Everyone needs to speak about this incident from their own position.

Roles might include the boy or girl who threw the stones, the parent of that child, the pensioner who was present, the chairperson of the centre, the glazier employed to fix the window, the yoga teacher who runs classes, the policeman who was called and the local youth worker.

Invite statements from each of the characters.

Then set up dialogues between characters; for example, child and parent, policeman and youth worker, or pensioner and glazier. This can be done either within the circle of chairs, or by moving to a stage.

Benefits of the Game

Articulacy, recognising other's viewpoints.

Variations and Extensions

If the exercise goes well thus far, more complex improvisations can be set up, arising out of the initial dialogues. This would involve staged scenes such as the incident itself or a backstory scene between the youth worker and the child that led to the child's disaffection.

Players	Age	Time
6+	14+	30

Negotiation

SKILLS – Negotiation

Taxi Ride

What are your options when you have no money and there's someone sat there demanding it?

How to Play

This is a staged problem-solving exercise, so most of the group will be watching as spectators.

Ask for two volunteers.

Two adjacent chairs are placed for them on the stage, facing the audience.

One is a taxi driver, one a passenger.

They are arriving at the passenger's destination, which is an empty warehouse where the passenger is employed as a security guard.

The problem is that the taxi driver's initial estimate of an £8 ride was inaccurate. He's now saying that it was a £12 ride.

The passenger only has £8 and no access to further money.

The task for the players is to work out a compromise or solution to the conflict between them so that no one player is disadvantaged. A 'promise to pay back' shouldn't really be allowed as it can't be judged whether that would happen. The solution should be found in the present rather than deferred to the future. It might involve objects given in part exchange, favours granted like a wash of the car or a cup of tea made, and so on.

Afterwards, the spectators judge whether or not a compromise has been achieved that is fair to both sides.

Benefits of the Game

Skills in compromise, listening, articulacy.

Players	Age	Time
6+	16+	10

The Jobsworth Line

Sometimes the shortest journey takes the longest time.

How to Play

Create a line of players standing across the room.

The task for a single player is to deliver an item to the player at the farthest end of the line. However, this can only be done by the player going through all the other players first in order to deliver it. The player doesn't know what tasks this will involve. He or she only finds out during the exercise. For example:

- The first in the line asks for a form P21, which can only be got from the fourth player in the line.

- The fourth player explains that he or she can grant a P21 but only with an XJ12 which is available from the second player.

- The second in line has to check the player's pockets for weapons, then instruct the player that he or she needs to deposit his or her shoes with the third player and come back with a chit saying this has been done.

- The third player takes the shoes and gives a chit.

- The player can then go to the second player, give the chit and receive an XJ12 to take to the fourth player and receive a P21 in return.

- Then the player can take this P21 to the first player in line who writes on it, gives it back and instructs it be taken to the fifth player in the line along with the item that needs to be given by the player making the journey.

The instructions for players could either be worked out in advance by the facilitator (preferred) – or improvised (if the group can be trusted to do this).

Benefits of the Game

Managing emotions, patience, problem-solving.

+ Paper, pens		
Players	**Age**	**Time**
6+	14+	10

Both Want the Car

It's about the baggage.

How to Play

Ask for two volunteers willing to improvise in front of the group.

The task is for both players to find a compromise to the problem within the scene, with neither player getting a worse deal.

The situation involves a father and teenage son (or mother and daughter). It's the father's car. Both want it that evening. The parent wants to go to a card game in the local town, the teenager to take out a girl (or boy). The father's event starts at 9 p.m. and finishes at 10. The son has arranged to meet the girl at 7 p.m. They plan to go to a film and return at around 11 p.m.

It's ten miles to the town and there's no transport.

The two players have to work out a solution which is satisfactory to both.

An example solution might be for the parent to drive the teenager to his or her date, return home then go out again. Then after the card game, to spend an hour doing something different so they can both come back together at 11 p.m. But this is rather in the teenager's favour. So what can be done for the parent? The parent might reasonably demand either payment for petrol or an embargo on use of the car for a month.

Benefits of the Game

Problem-solving skills, listening skills, communication skills.

Players	Age	Time
6+	14+	10

Blue Room, Green Room

When both parties have completely different recollections of what was said.

How to Play

Ask for two volunteers to improvise in front of the group.

They have the task of finding a solution to a problem without one or the other being overly disadvantaged.

One has employed the other to paint a room in a house due to be used as an office.

The room has now been painted.

When the owner arrives back, he or she finds it's been painted the wrong colour. The owner recalls clearly giving an instruction to paint the room blue. But it's green. The painter distinctly remembers being told to paint the room green. Paint was bought accordingly.

How to resolve the problem? The owner wants the room blue, that's certain. But given the painter is working by the hour and has now completed six hours, who is to pay the wage if the room is repainted?

A compromise might, for example, involve a lower hourly rate or the owner helping with the painting.

Benefits of the Game

Problem-solving skills, communication skills.

Players	Age	Time
6+	14+	10

The Wedding Funeral

When opposites collide.

How to Play

Ask for two volunteers willing to improvise in front of the group.

Their task is to find a solution to a problem without either one being overly disadvantaged.

They are playing two strangers who find they have both booked the same function room for the same time: a Saturday afternoon. They both arrive earlier in the day to find the other one in there. It appears they have both made separate arrangements with the same administrator to use the room at the same time; one for a wake (party after a funeral), one for a wedding party.

The task is to work out a compromise arrangement.

There are no other spaces available and the administrator cannot be contacted. In both cases, guests have been given the details of the venue and are due to arrive in a few hours' time.

A solution might involve a splitting of the time available or perhaps the mourners might be persuaded to look on death as a cause for celebration of life (I've yet to hear this proposed…).

Benefits of the Game

Listening, problem-solving skills.

Players	Age	Time
6+	14+	10

Drunk on the Bus

Dealing with the unwelcome attentions of a drunk.

How to Play

For this exercise you need an actor, facilitator or group member who can play a drunk character sensitively within a role-play structure.

The setting is a bus, tube or other enclosed public place from which there is no immediate escape.

The task for the volunteer or challenger is to deal with the behaviour of this drunk character, who has little respect for personal space.

Prime the actor playing the drunk beforehand as to how to play the scene. The action of this character should be insistent, but giving due response to the dexterity with which the other player is dealing with the problem.

Instruct the volunteer to sit in the location that has been created with chairs. The actor playing the drunk then arrives and tries to engage the other player in conversation. This might involve sitting next to the player and/or breaking into that player's personal space.

There may be some physical contact although this should never become sexual (because that takes the exercise into another territory). The physical contact is purely non-aggressive and 'friendly'.

The volunteer's task is to be polite and to avoid swearing or using physical aggression while keeping the drunk at bay.

The rest of the group should be invited for their comments after the improvisation is over. How was the problematic behaviour of the drunk dealt with? What else could have been done?

Benefits of the Game

Awareness of personal strategies in situations of discomfort, communication skills.

Players	Age	Time
6+	14+	15

Three Nations

A miniaturised version of an exercise on cooperation and conflict I developed for the British Council.

How to Play

Divide everyone into three groups, 1, 2 and 3.

Give each group the same quantity of different items; these items represent different kinds of wealth:

- Item A is a small plastic container representing a barrel of oil.
- B is a pencil representing tools.
- C is a sweet representing food.

So group 1 gets twenty barrels of oil, group 2 twenty tools, and group 3 twenty food packages.

You could alternatively use different coloured tokens.

The task for each group is to negotiate with each other, so that at the end of the game, wealth has been accumulated through trade. The aim is to get as much as possible of the different currencies. An equal amount of oil, tools and food would represent a 'balanced' or 'mixed' economy.

Just to make things more interesting, and to give a chance for one team to be clear winners, there is a gambling table run by one of the facilitators. He or she sits there with a pack of cards and represents 'the bank'. Banking practice in this game is pretty unreliable. A player can go to the table and gamble any number of items. How it works is the banker deals him or herself a card and the visitor a card. If the visitor is in a winning position with the higher-value card, he or she doubles whatever stake was risked. This wealth is drawn from the bank. If they are in a losing position, the visitor loses the stake. The banker may also offer other kinds of gambles – or these may be requested. For example, if the visitor gambles one unit, this could be trebled if the team player can answer a general-knowledge question. If the visitor wins, the reward is three units of choice.

The team with the most wealth at the end of a period of time, perhaps half an hour, is the winner.

A scoring system needs to be worked out in advance so that, for example, while a point is scored for each item held at the end, extra points are given to those teams that have a balanced economy.

Benefits of the Game

Working with calculation, estimating risk, combining teamwork with competitiveness.

Note

There's plenty of scope in the exercise for it to be tailored to the group for whom it's intended by, for example, modifying the extent of complexity or by structuring the role of the banker. A greater or smaller emphasis can be given to the opportunity to 'beat the banker', either by answering general-knowledge questions or by other means, such as answering maths puzzles without the use of a calculator.

In a longer version of this exercise the three nations are given a political system of government, which means that decisions about trading have to be made collectively, autocratically or anarchistically. Finally, there can be a fourth, rogue state that trades in arms.

+ Small containers, pencils and sweets or tokens, pack of cards		
Players	**Age**	**Time**
12+	14+	45

Performance

SKILLS – Performance

Reactions

It's said that acting is fundamentally only reacting.

How to Play

Organise the group into a standing circle.

One player stands in the middle of the circle.

A player from the circle comes into the middle and gives the centre player some news to react to.

Rules can be laid down about the news. For example, it should not involve death or disease. Insults are proscribed. So *'You're about to die from cancer'* doesn't really get the party going, but *'I'm pregnant'*, while being something of a stock subject in youth theatre, is certainly fine (less so for boys).

The centre player then gives a reaction to the news, and takes an opportunity to exit the stage.

The reaction might involve pleasure, indifference, excitement, despair, anger, horror, joy or something else entirely. It should be spontaneous.

The player who brought the news stays on. Another player jumps in with some different news.

Generally, the news should come from the world of fiction. It should be made up. *'Your cat just died'* – if it is known that the player has a cat – may be a little unfair.

Benefits of the Game

It starts getting players comfortable with saying the first thing that comes to mind. It gives them a chance to be funny within a short time frame, without pulling the improvisation into a comedy graveyard.

Variations and Extensions

There's the possibility of asking the players to extend the dialogue into a scene. This might be extended further by the introduction of other characters.

Players	Age	Time
8+	**8+**	**15**

Following

A short game followed by an improvisation.

How to Play

Divide the group into pairs.

Ask each pair to have a walker and a follower.

The walker is simply to walk about the space, the follower is to follow.

Initially, the follower should play at avoiding being seen. (Although obviously both players know what is going on.)

Now and again the walker can turn around suddenly, in which case the follower has to pretend to be doing something completely different.

Finally, the walker turns around suddenly and catches the follower out. The next question is *'Why are you following me?'* The answer needs to be spontaneous. It should be improvised in the moment, allowing a dialogue to flow from there. What the follower must not do is deny that he or she has been following.

A good way to run the exercise is for the pairs to run it once, then everyone comes together and players talk about what happened. There's an opportunity then to make a few points about how this kind of improvisation works best. For example, it makes more sense for the follower to be candid and confessional. It creates a more interesting drama that way, and allows a relationship to develop. Nonsense answers or blanket denials tend not to lead anywhere.

Benefits of the Game

It offers a way into improvisation and encourages an understanding that improvisation relies on self-disclosure.

Players	Age	Time
6+	14+	10

Two People Meet

An exercise that starts simply and can extend into more and more complexity.

How to Play

Organise the group to sit in a large circle, with plenty of stage space in the middle.

Ask everyone to choose for themselves a partner across the circle. Everyone should have one partner only; however, if there are uneven numbers, then someone might have two partners.

The rule is, if your partner gets up, then you have to.

Start by asking everyone to change places with their partner – but in doing so there should not be more than two people crossing the circle at the same time.

When everyone has crossed, move to the next stage.

Now everyone has to cross but say '*Hi*' to their partner as they cross. Again, no more than two crossing at any one time. Other than that, people can go in any order.

The third time of crossing, one player has to ask the other a question to which the answer must be '*No*'.

The fourth time, the answer must be '*Yes*'.

Whenever a pair gets up, it's not established before they meet who will be the asker and who will answer.

The next time, more tailored instructions can be given. These can get progressively more complex; the aim is to trigger improvisations. (The meetings are always accidental unless otherwise stated.)

For example:

- Two people meet. One owes the other money but doesn't have any.

- Two people meet. They were both at a party last night and one of them behaved really badly, but can't remember what happened.

- Two people meet. They used to be friends but something happened and they haven't spoken for a while.

- Two people meet. They used to be best friends but one developed a drug problem and the other became very successful.

- Two people meet. They are brother and sister but only one has been in touch with the family recently.

Almost certainly the facilitator will need to be ready to sort out problems that arise, such as the task not being addressed or improvisational offers being avoided or blocked. It's an exercise that will benefit from what is sometimes called 'side-coaching', the facilitator giving further instructions or advice while the improvisations are running.

Benefits of the Game

Becoming used to increasingly complex improvisational challenges, learning the basic conventions of improvisation; saying 'Yes', accepting other's inventions and dealing with awkwardness.

Note

The duration of the game can be judged according to the ability of the players. Similarly, the instruction to 'keep it short' protects those who are not yet confident.

Players	Age	Time
8+	14+	30

SKILLS – Performance

First Lines of Scenes

Often the most difficult part of improvisation is getting started.

How to Play

Divide the group into pairs.

Explain that each pair will do an improvisation or scene between them. There's no need to establish in advance what the relationship is or who these characters are; the aim is to find out as they go along.

All the pairs can improvise simultaneously, each in their own space. Players should follow their instincts – once the opening line has been given.

First lines might be:

- 'Where were you last night?'
- 'You're late for work again, I see!'
- 'So what did you say happened to my dog exactly?'
- 'So – did you manage to break into the house?'
- 'Habib, I think this ship is going down.'
- 'Why does this boy keep phoning you?'

Clearly these can be written to suit the group in question, tapping into their likely concerns or interests.

Players should be encouraged to let the dialogue go where it will. *But* players should be discouraged from simply having an argument or just being negative towards each other. If this happens, better to ask the pair in question to stop and start again with a new first line.

Benefits of the Game

Encourages awareness that what is funny, spiteful or negative doesn't necessarily develop a good scene; encourages an understanding that drama develops well if there is revelation or confession involved.

Variations and Extensions

It's often best for the exercise to be played initially by pairs on their own, then if it's going well enough, for pairs to be invited to play out new scenes (or even repeat old ones) in front of an audience (the rest of the group).

Note

The 'first line' is essentially an offer, in the traditional impro sense. And like all offers onstage, it's not good or bad in itself. It's the response that's important. The responding player always needs to seek out the opportunities generated, avoiding the temptation to blame the other players for a bad line.

Players	Age	Time
8+	10+	20

Blind Offers

A classic exercise from the influential and ever-inventive Keith Johnstone.

How to Play

Organise the group into pairs.

The pairs should find themselves a space each.

One player in each pair is asked to make a still, physical shape.

The other player is going to react to it. The way to react to it is by imagining what's going on: 'Who might the other player be, and who could I be?'

Then to start improvising on the basis of answers found.

The first player needs to accept the decisions made by the second player, and play along.

The possibilities are without limit so I won't list any. On the other hand… I can imagine two drunk flies trying to escape from honey; a Member of Parliament in a bar confessing to sin; two cowboys about to fight their last gun battle; a camel and its owner parting company after all these years; Jesus finally finding the woman of his dreams; the winner of a parsnip-eating competition consoling the one who came second…

Okay, that's enough.

Players should be encouraged to keep the scene short, concluding it and then changing over.

After some practice, the exercise can be run in front of the audience (but insist on playing new scenes, not repeating old ones).

Benefits of the Game

Finding out what encourages collaboration between players – and what inhibits it.

Note

Players will often fall into playing 'teaching scenes', where one player instructs the other – or 'art scenes', where someone pretends to be a piece of art. Or there may be scenes where someone has a physical injury or is stuck in a crack in the pavement. Scenes like these are often defaults for learners, and can be welcomed on that basis, but it may be a good idea to allow only one teaching, dancing or injury scene per spell of play.

There'll also be a lot of miming of objects, which is sometimes a way to shift focus away from physicality. My approach is not to disallow it but to commend the scenes that eschew mime more highly, and simply observe the limitations of those that don't.

The legacy of 'comedy impro' is not always a beneficial one. People often try too hard to be funny. So they habitually avoid seeing what might be an obvious but nevertheless more 'real' and 'playable' situation in front of them.

As Keith Johnstone has himself observed, if the effort to be funny is more visible than the comedy, you're pointing in the wrong direction.

Players	Age	Time
6+	12+	20

The Bridge

An exercise developed by RG Gregory to ensure that authorship in play-making is shared democratically.

How to Play

This exercise assumes an initial level of ability and some measure of self-discipline. If group members can work responsibly on their own, this is a good exercise. You need four or eight or perhaps sixteen in the group – otherwise the maths are at odds with the process.

Propose or request a theme for the exercise. Don't accept a theme proposal if it isn't a strong one. The test is, does the theme suggest scenes and stories? 'Drugs' does, 'Violence' does, 'The Moon' does, 'Conflict' doesn't – it's too broad and also generic – and 'Shakespeare' doesn't – he's a guy, not a theme.

Ask everyone in the group to find a space on their own and to create a short piece of dramatic action by themselves. It can be very short. For their action, each player needs to define who they are, where they are and what they are doing. The action can be mundane or dramatic – but it must in some way connect to the theme. Using mime is okay, although it's best done without. Props, if available, are to be preferred.

For example, the theme is 'Flight'. One player, Sean, decides to be a zookeeper hiding from a lion that's escaped. His activity is running and then jumping into a hiding place. The second player, Samantha, has decided to be a girl travelling alone in an aeroplane to meet her father abroad for the first time. She's painting her nails.

Everyone prepares their short scenes at the same time.

Then all the players team up in pairs. In each pair, players perform their pieces to each other. Then each pair has to work out how their two pieces can be made to connect. To achieve this, they devise a 'bridge section' which might come either between their two pieces, or before both or after both.

If the first player, Sean, is the zookeeper and the second, Samantha, is the girl doing her nails, then how can these scenes be joined? Maybe the zookeeper is the girl's father. So the bridge piece in this case might be Samantha visiting Sean in hospital after his arm's been chewed off.

When these two players have created their joined-up drama with both their initial sections and a bridge section in it, they rehearse it, then team up with another pair (who also has a similar length piece of drama) and work out how their respective longer pieces can be combined.

You might want to stop there and have all those pieces of drama presented: each short play should have four characters in it. Or you might go further and create a play with eight characters.

Benefits of the Game

Collaboration, use of storylines, lateral thinking.

Note

Once a piece of action is created, then major changes to it are pretty much disallowed (part of the challenge is working with the inherited fabric – it also protects the creativity of individuals), but minor accommodations are fine.

What's important is that the integrity of the democratic structure is respected.

+ Assorted props		
Players	**Age**	**Time**
4 or 8 or 16	12+	40

SKILLS – Performance

Park Bench

Thanks to Divian Ladwa for showing me how to make this one work.

How to Play

Set up some chairs to look like a park bench.

Explain that the group is going to improvise a series of encounters on this bench. Different people are going to meet; some will be strangers to each other, some will know each other.

Ask for one player to sit on the bench.

Another player goes to sit on the bench shortly afterwards.

The instruction is simply for the players to make some decisions about what their relationship is. If strangers, they might strike up a dialogue or ignore each other. If they know each other, then *how* they know each other needs to be made clear.

All the good behaviours of improvisation are to be encouraged: listening to the other person, not contradicting the other person, not having an argument, accepting what the other person says to be true.

After a while, the first player leaves the bench.

Then another arrives and meets the second person.

This should be a different kind of relationship. It could alternate; a stranger relationship followed by a pre-existing relationship followed by strangers, etc.

The facilitator can interrupt with suggestions or instructions to keep the action developing.

Benefits of the Game

Listening, cooperating, using imagination.

Players	Age	Time
6+	12+	15

Two Rush In

Every sitcom ever made has a scene when someone –
or some two – rush in and tell their friends about some
extraordinary event that's just been witnessed.

How to Play

Request two volunteers to perform.

Ask them to imagine that they've just seen
something amazing. It probably happened in the
corridor, on the street or on the bus.

The two players are going to tell the story of what
happened to the rest of the group.

The best way to play the scene is not to plan the
story but just go for it. Encourage them to rush in
and start talking very fast. Give them the first line,
something like:

> 'You won't believe what just happened. We *saw this*
> *extraordinary –* '

Then ask the other player to take it up.

> ' *– elephant walking along the street. It had –* '

> ' *– ears as big as –* '

> ' *– trees –* '

If necessary, point at each of the players alternately
to direct the storytelling.

It doesn't matter how fantastical the story is as long
as they agree with and reinforce each other.

Encourage them to come to an end when the story
feels complete.

Benefits of the Game

Teamwork, imagination, storytelling.

Variations and Extensions

An alternative strategy would be to allow the
players to plan in advance the core idea of the
event they witnessed. Or an event idea could be
given to them.

Players	Age	Time
4+	12+	10

SKILLS – Performance

Selling

For the business-minded, selling may be easier than acting.

How to Play

You need a good collection of props; if possible it should include some abstract pieces of wood, plastic or metal.

Divide the group into pairs.

Ask each pair to pick an item from the props collection. Something that intrigues them.

Explain they should prepare to sell this item to the rest of the group as if in a market situation. They can 'endow' this object as anything they like (assume it has properties the real object doesn't have), but it does need to have a clear function. It might remove unwanted hair or frighten reindeer from your lawn, or it might be effective at hypnotising the girlfriend or boyfriend of your dreams.

Each pair prepares a sales pitch. The partners also need to work out their separate roles in presenting the pitch. It might be as simple as a seller and an assistant. It's the seller who demonstrates the item while calling the price, while the assistant takes orders. The core of the scene is the demonstration, which can be highly theatrical.

Then the group assembles and each pair sells in turn.

The audience may need to be instructed not to turn negative on the sellers. The idea may be strange or ridiculous, but the audience still needs to act interested, ask questions and buy!

Benefits of the Game

Communication skills, use of imagination, teamwork, dealing with hecklers.

+ Assorted props		
Players	**Age**	**Time**
6+	12+	15

PART FIVE

CHALLENGES

Setting Up Challenges

This chapter sets out a number of challenge exercises of potentially varying length. There is a different social or problem-solving skill being tested in each one, although inevitably the more complex exercises do tax a range of skills and abilities. They were largely devised by Saul Hewish and myself for young men in prison, with a view to the fact they would soon be leaving and facing challenges in the outside world. (This is why the challenger is always referred to as 'he' – although there is no intention to imply that the exercises can't be made suitable for a female group.) In almost all cases, challenges were devised in the first instance for specific individuals, before later becoming staple exercises used for a wider number of inmates. Whatever the gestation, it's always the case that a challenge exercise functions entirely for the benefit of one individual only. Everyone else in the group is collaborating with that objective in mind.

There is a set of procedures that we devised for these challenges, which may be worth following or at least being aware of, simply because they help with the efficacy of the exercises. The challenge would always be prepared on the basis of knowledge of the particular individual and how he needed to be tested. For example, participant A has issues controlling anger, while B has poor interpersonal skills or communicates ineffectively. The use of these procedures was always a key ingredient in any successful piece of work.

First, the facilitators devise the scenario in private, probably the day before. Once in the session, the set-up needs to be explained to the group with the challenger outside the space. This is because the value of the challenge lies partly in the surprise element. The preparation involves explaining the devised scenario and probably enlisting members of the group to play specific roles within it. The success of the challenge does depend in part upon how well these roles are played. If they're played badly, the challenge falls to the ground with collective sighs of disappointment or irritation. If the facilitating team includes actors, therefore, they should be cast into roles first. These roles are likely to include family, friends, managers, customers, workers and so on. The central role is of course played by the challenger.

Let's imagine there's a challenger called Dave. It's important that Dave understands he must play *himself* in this challenge. He's not playing a fictional character, even though everyone around him *is* playing fictional characters. Dave's role is not about *creating drama*, it's not about generating an exciting story for the sake of the audience. A successful challenge can very likely be something of a dull watch for the spectators.

Dave needs to deal with the problems as best he can while avoiding breaking the law and resorting to violence. Now, in respect of the fictional elements, there will be facts that Dave as the challenger will need to be told. For example, that he, Dave, has started working in a burger bar or that he has an old relative called Auntie May. He's going for flying lessons or needs to find a place to live. If any of these made-up facts seriously conflicts with the real story of Dave's life or his future plans, then they should be altered so they fit. If Dave hates meat and would never work in a burger bar or recently lost a grandparent, then for different reasons these two fictional elements should be altered. A certain amount of checking facts in advance with Dave will therefore be necessary. It's also important not to give Dave a backstory that involves him having already broken the law, as this would clearly put him at an unfair disadvantage come the exercise. Much of this can be sorted out with Dave outside the room, while inside the challenge is being set up.

As indicated previously, Dave is told nothing of what is going to happen. The group should work together under the facilitator's direction to present and maintain a sequence of provocations that are embedded within the improvisation that unfolds.

Those playing the other roles should understand as far as possible how their playing will test Dave. They should be encouraged to respond positively if Dave presents an intelligent or effective strategy, but be willing to offer resistance or raise the stakes if he doesn't. They should not simply focus on trying to defeat the challenger – that's not the purpose of the drama. If one of the supporting characters invites him outside to rearrange his features and he refuses, he can't simply be dragged out there.

The role play may run over several scenes. It may last anything from a few minutes to half an hour or more depending on the complexity of the challenge and the challenger's response to it. If Dave feels at any time that he actually can't think of any course of action other than violence or law-breaking, he should stop the challenge and make that clear. We have known it happen on a few occasions. If this happens, there's an option of restarting the challenge if a different way forward has been identified through discussion.

Dave may also choose to take 'time out' at any point – in which case the challenge is suspended while he has an opportunity to review his options. This doesn't extend to asking for advice. It's simply a private moment to reflect before re-entering the fray. It's equivalent to 'stopping time' and reclaiming the practice of thought.

The facilitator's task is to manage the drama, noting the choices made by the challenger and moving the scenes along, changing the location and time of the drama where necessary. New, unanticipated characters can always be introduced. If the scenario started with Dave working in a burger bar, but he decides that he wants to leave the bar to avoid a fight, and goes to a pub, then the location might be moved to the pub. Drinkers or a landlord may be needed. One of them might need to take the role of a provocateur in the evolving situation, offering a further challenge to Dave's propensity for getting into arguments.

There should always be a clear focus to the overall challenge; for example, it's about Dave learning to manage his emotions, especially anger – so the facilitator will be looking to maintain the scenario in such a way that this issue remains alive. If going to the pub means Dave abandons the job, thereby putting it on the line, we might move to the next day and run a scene where his manager gives him something of a dressing-down – to see how Dave handles it.

Dave should similarly be clear in his own mind what his general objective is in the challenge, i.e. to keep his job at the burger bar while avoiding fights. But the latter is by far the most important and should be understood as such, since it's getting into fights rather than being unemployed that led him to prison. So if he loses the job but stays out of trouble, that may represent a good result for Dave.

Feedback and post-show discussion are not just important but essential. The challenger needs to hear from the facilitators and the rest of the group their observations on how well he did. It's also an opportunity for him to share the thoughts and feelings he had during the piece, without which it's harder for the facilitators to make any kind of full assessment.

It's always useful to start with positives, observing what Dave did well, even though he might have struggled throughout. Then the chat can move on to what he might have done differently, as well as questioning Dave on his own assessment of himself. Young guys in prison may well be pretty locked down in terms of what they are prepared to talk about, so it makes sense to be both patient as well as challenging. The challenger, in this case Dave, may need a little time to open up. The process can be helped if the rest of the group are contributing to it in a positive way. Links can be made to Dave's personal history of offending if it's known and if that's appropriate.

Mediation Skills

The following scenarios call for the challenger to
demonstrate skills in:

- Seeing things from different perspectives
- Intervening to reduce conflict
- Keeping a sense of priorities

The Stolen Jacket

Can you stay calm and objective when your friend is losing the plot? The focus here is on reducing conflict.

Set-Up

The challenger has a friend; it might be either a mate or possibly a girlfriend. The point is, this friend was at a party last night – he or she went alone – and left a jacket behind in the house. It was a special jacket; it cost a lot of money. It might have been a gift from a family member.

On the day after the party, the two have an arrangement to go off to an event, but the challenger's friend wants to call in to the house where the party was to collect the jacket. They plan to travel in the challenger's car (assuming the challenger is a driver in real life, otherwise it's the friend's car).

Characters (besides the challenger)

• Girlfriend or mate

• Guy who lives in the party flat

The two group members playing these characters need to be briefed so they understand they have to work together to create a dilemma for the challenger. Essentially, the challenger should be caught in a tug of war between the jacket owner, who wants the jacket back at all costs, and the party host, who is denying all knowledge of it (but has probably given it away to someone else at the end of the party, or has hidden it).

Locations

• Car in which the pair travel to the party house and in which they intend to travel on to the event

• Front room of the house in which the party was held

Challenge

When they arrive, the occupant who held the party claims he doesn't know about any jacket. Nor is there evidence of it in the flat. The jacket owner insists he or she left it there. Perhaps, the host suggests, it might have been thrown into the rubbish late last night but sadly the bins have already been cleared.

The occupant should offer his guests a drink and go out to get it. While he's out of the room, the friend asks the challenger to search the flat since the friend is convinced their host is lying. Or the friend can simply start searching the place regardless. Either tactic will put the challenger under pressure.

The host returns to catch one of the two rifling through the room's contents or looking into cupboards. The host becomes angry. The friend starts accusing the host of stealing the jacket and concealing it deliberately. In return, the party host can make jibes at the friend over getting too wasted the night before and becoming forgetful.

It can come to direct confrontation between them.

It's the challenger's job to intervene in the conflict and steer the other parties towards a resolution.

Some conclusion to the conflict needs be found.

The stakes can always be raised by a traffic warden outside (in another part of the space), placing a ticket on the challenger's car.

Evaluation

- What means did the challenger use to mediate in the situation?
- Were these successful? If not, why not?
- Where there any other strategies that could have been used?
- Did the challenger become drawn in himself?

Evaluation shouldn't focus on what other characters might have done; it has to concentrate on the challenger. In this exercise, things may well hinge on whether or not he can get the friend to accept that the jacket is now lost. It should be evident that the host's word is not to be trusted, but the problem is, without involving the police or forcibly initiating a search, there is no further, useful way of challenging this dishonesty.

The Chat-Up

For a male challenger and a mixed-gender team. The focus here is on defining priorities in the situation and using reasonableness to defuse a conflict.

Set-Up

In this challenge, there's a girlfriend who needs to be played by one of the facilitators.

Characters

- Mate
- Couple not known to the challenger
- Other drinkers
- Barman (on standby)

Location

- Pub with drink, etc.

Challenge

The challenger has gone to the pub with his (male) friend. After some chat, the friend goes off to play pool.

A man and a woman, a couple, arrive together. Then the man goes out to the toilet. The woman turns to the challenger and starts chatting with him. The aim for her is just to involve him in chat; nothing serious, just banter.

Then her boyfriend comes back and stands for a moment, watching this conversation. He then comes over and demands that the girlfriend step aside to have a conversation. She does this and he launches a tirade at her. He's clearly jealous and angry that she should talk to anyone else. She should say that the other man – the challenger – initiated the conversation. So then the boyfriend goes over to the challenger and has a go at him as well.

At this point the challenger's friend should return and get involved, standing up for his friend and stirring the pot.

The challenger's task is to try and lower the temperature, preventing a fight and getting everyone back to their pints.

Evaluation

- What techniques did the challenger use to defuse the conflict and were they effective?

- Is there anything else that could have been tried?

- How did the challenger respond as the situation didn't go the way he expected?

- What were the thoughts and feelings of the challenger throughout?

- What's the role of sexual jealousy in arguments between men?

The Old People's Home

Sometimes it's not the young but the old who are the most troublesome. Here the focus is on using diplomacy and restraint.

Set-Up

For this challenge, you need a small portable radio.

The challenger has a relative, an old man or woman – let's say an uncle for this example – who's stuck in an old people's home. Every so often someone from the family has to go and visit him. This time it's the challenger's turn. As with all these exercises, it's important the relationships are clearly understood before the challenge begins.

Characters

- Old uncle
- Manager and other staff working in the home

Locations

- Recreation area in an old people's home
- Staff office

Challenge

When the challenger arrives, he is told by the uncle that *'These people have got it in for me.'* The uncle claims that *'They stole my radio'* and asks *'Can you get it back for me?'*

When the challenger goes to the manager, assuming he does, he learns what happened; that the radio was confiscated because the uncle was playing it too loud and disturbing the other residents. And it can't be given back.

This then is the conflict that the challenger has to mediate between his uncle and the institution.

The uncle's next strategy might be to ask his nephew or niece to steal the radio back. Or possibly to try and steal it himself while the manager is preoccupied. He might request the challenger distract the staff, allowing him to do this.

As with other challenges, the drama can be organised so that the challenger has a continuing set of difficulties to resolve. The uncle, for example, can have privileges removed from him in consequence for his bad behaviour.

Evaluation

- What kind of relationship did the challenger establish with the uncle?
- How did the challenger deal with the manager while representing the uncle's case?
- How effective was the challenger in mediating in this conflict?
- Did the situation improve or was it made worse?

Forged Tickets

Nothing is more frustrating than expectation denied at the very last minute. Here the focus is on managing the heightened emotions of a friend whose behaviour will likely get them both into trouble.

Set-Up

The challenger has a friend. Paper money is needed for this scenario and it needs to be carefully given out.

The two friends are due to go to an event (concert, gig, football match – check that the challenger would in real life be happy to go to whatever is chosen).

Characters

- Friend
- Ticket seller
- Steward/bouncer
- Man with forged tickets
- Barman/woman
- People in the queue (if required)

Locations

- Outside the event
- Pub

Challenge

The challenger and his friend go to buy tickets at the event, but it's sold out. Their frustration will be heightened if they have to wait in a queue before they find this out.

The challenger's friend suggests they go for a drink instead.

In the pub, someone comes round the tables offering to sell two tickets for the same event. The challenger's friend urges they buy.

Assuming they do – handing over paper money – they go back to the concert and try to get in with the tickets. However, the steward identifies the tickets as forged and refuses to let them in. The friend insists they return to the pub to find the seller.

This is the moment of difficulty for the challenger. If he goes back, which is likely, the seller should be there and should refuse to pay the money on the grounds that he himself paid good money for them. It's not his fault if they were forged.

The friend can raise the stakes by suggesting that the two of them, he and the challenger, take revenge on the ticket seller by robbing him or beating him up. The friend needs to present himself as someone who is extremely angry and would be happy to break the law to get revenge.

The challenger needs to defuse the situation and avoid either violence or law-breaking.

Evaluation

• At which points did the challenger face difficult decisions?

• Did the challenger make decisions or avoid them?

• What tactics were tried and how successful were they?

The Couple Who Argue

There's nothing quite as intractable as a private squabble. Here the focus is on keeping a cool head and not getting drawn into taking sides.

Set-Up

The challenger has been asked to do some temporary work for a couple who are reorganising their house. If necessary, this can be established during an initial scene in which the challenger goes for a job and is offered good money for a week's work helping a couple do the reorganising. The payment is by the hour.

Characters

• Argumentative couple

Location

• Couple's house

Challenge

When the challenger arrives, one of the couple meets him and explains what is involved in the reorganisation.

There needs to be a good supply of furniture in the room for this exercise.

Houseowner 1 explains that the challenger needs to move the furniture to help the couple decide how they want it. He or she proposes a particular arrangement and the challenger is asked to move furniture accordingly.

Then houseowner 2 arrives and complains that this is not what was previously agreed. He or she instructs the challenger to move the furniture around again.

Soon the couple are arguing between themselves, in front of the challenger. Each one makes different demands of him.

Does the challenger offer any advice or try to help?

Finally, the couple get to the point where they refuse to speak to each other. They will only communicate to the other party via the challenger, who then has to relay messages between them.

To conclude, the challenger is accused of making things worse and possibly of causing the conflict in the first place.

Of course the challenger can simply walk out, but what other strategies are available?

Evaluation

- Did the challenger make the situation better or worse?

- What strategies were used?

- Could the challenger have been more persuasive?

- Did the challenger become emotionally involved even though the arrangement of the furniture wasn't exactly his problem?

Communication Skills

The following scenarios call for the challenger to demonstrate skills in:

- Articulacy
- Summarising a problem
- Transmitting information
- Assertiveness

The Chairs

Working for an authority at odds with itself is like trying to get a snake to play piano. The focus here is on not getting frustrated, and finding strategies to solve the problem.

Set-Up

The challenger has recently been given a job working at a conference centre as a porter.

His job is to move chairs and prepare rooms for business meetings, etc. There are two managers to whom the challenger is accountable.

Characters

• Two managers

Location

• Room in a conference centre

Challenge

The challenger is called to a room by Manager 1 and asked to organise the chairs in rows, all facing towards a table. The visiting physicians are holding a lecture, he says. Manager 1 then leaves.

Manager 2 arrives and tells the challenger that this is all wrong. The chairs need to be put in a circle. The visiting physicians are having a discussion. Manager 2 then leaves.

Manager 1 returns and is angry to find that the challenger has moved the chairs into the wrong position.

This can continue indefinitely.

How does the challenger deal with the problem?

Can he get the two parties talking to each other rather than dumping the problem on him?

Those playing the two managers need to improvise in order to keep the challenger guessing – and dealing with problems. But they should respond positively if the challenger comes up with a good strategy.

Evaluation

- At what point did the challenger stop simply obeying orders?
- What initiative did the challenger take to resolve the problem?
- What other tactics might have been used?
- To what extent did the challenger allow the problems in the situation to get on top of him?
- Even though others are clearly at fault, was he able to act like a responsible employee?

The Christmas Present

I developed this exercise initially for a guy who used to roll up to his probation group in a white Mercedes, boasting that he was the great provider for his community... he improbably claimed that money wasn't important in his life. The focus here is on humility.

Set-Up

The exercise is really about being humble; being willing to accept your limitations to your own family. The context is Christmas and a boy who wants a particular present very badly. The challenger needs to be old enough to have a six- or seven-year-old child.

Characters

- Son or daughter
- Mother or older son
- Salesperson
- Telephonist at the store
- Customers at the store

Locations

- Living room
- Possibly a department store, toy section

Challenge

Being two days before Christmas, the son or daughter comes to the father with a request for a Christmas present. It's something he wants a lot. It's a Flaxhollinger 2.5 which is currently very popular with six-year-olds. (I just made that up so don't look for it.)

The actor playing the child will be trying to get an assurance from the parent that this toy *will* be found for him.

The suggestion is made to the challenger that he might like to go and buy this for his son from a store where the toy is stocked. Suggest he might like to ring the store first.

Assuming he calls up, the player on the phone at the store says yes, they have some of that toy in stock.

Assuming he then goes to the store, when he arrives, someone in front of him buys the last one.

There are no more of these toys anywhere.

The challenger has to go home and explain to the child that he wasn't able to get the toy (he can of course buy something else, but to the boy it isn't the same at all). He needs to be as frank as possible about what happened, and deal with the inevitable tantrum.

Evaluation

This would focus on how the challenger has dealt with the situation in terms of finding a balance between not hurting the son and telling the truth. It might also involve some recognition of a failure to plan sufficiently for Christmas, although it has to be said that this may be a tad unfair since he has been rather handed this predicament.

Variation

When the father arrives back after unsuccessfully visiting the shop, a parcel is delivered by the postman. On opening, it's the much-desired toy – however, there's a mistake and it's for the house next door. (This is apparent only once the parcel has been opened.) The boy has witnessed the opening and doesn't understand why he can't have the toy. Needless to say, he's pretty unhappy and wants to make a scene about it: '*Daddy doesn't love me…*'

CHALLENGES – Communication

The Youth Club

This is a tough challenge for any young adult with the capacity for leadership. The focus here is on caution.

Set-Up

The context is a youth club which doesn't have a lot of money. However, £5,000 has just been raised successfully to spend within the club. At the same time, the club is taking on a new youth worker – this role is to be played by the challenger.

Characters

- Club manager
- Another youth worker (if required)
- Young people
- Youth club board members (if required)

Locations

- Different spaces in a youth club

Challenge

The new youth worker is brought into the manager's office and told something about the club. He's also told about the £5,000 to be spent. So to help build a relationship with the young people, the manager asks him to go and find out what the young people would like the money to be spent on. Anything is permissible as long as it can be spent (legally) on youth-club activities or equipment. The challenger is asked to bring the results back to the manager.

The task for those playing the young people is to give the challenger lots of conflicting ideas – forcing him to manage the situation and create priorities.

The new worker goes back to the manager and gives the results of the discussion with the young people. The suggestions might involve a go-kart track, basketball hoop, a pool table or other stuff.

Then there's an optional scene with some board members in which the ideas need to be presented by the new youth leader.

However, the board members agree that this proposed use is inappropriate for the money and it's better spent on cricket (for example) – something that the kids won't really like very much (but is good for them, allegedly).

If there is no board meeting, then the manager can simply bring the youth worker into the office and tell him the same news, it having come down from HQ.

The youth worker is then instructed by the manager to go and give the bad news to the young people, who naturally turn against him and blame him for building up their hopes.

Evaluation

• Did the challenger give a guarantee to the young people that he could deliver whatever they asked?

• How did the challenger react once the news came out that the money couldn't be spent as the young people wanted?

• Did the challenger involve the other youth worker or an area manager (if one had been cast in the challenge)?

Variation: Drugs in the Youth Club

In this version, the grant is a less important issue. On meeting the young people for the first time, the youth worker picks up from them that they are all sharing drugs. They also intimate to him that it's okay because John – the other youth worker – says it's okay. In fact, John sold them the drugs.

The challenge then becomes about how the new worker tackles John and/or the manager. John is a long-established youth worker who got the manager the job in the first place. So the manager doesn't want to move against him. If this scenario is followed, a possible course of action for the challenger would be to approach someone higher up in the Youth Service, in which case reference to an area manager might usefully be made by the manager in the first scene. Or the area manager might be present when the youth worker first arrives.

The Untrustworthy Partner

Professional standards may slip somewhat when your partner is trashing the job. The focus here is on assertiveness.

Set-Up

The challenger has recently acquired a job working for a firm of painters and decorators. (It may be useful to have some old paint cans for this scenario, but if unavailable, some stand-in props would do the job. A couple of 'breakable items' are also useful.)

The company always sends out workers in pairs. On the occasion of his first job, the challenger is to be sent out with the manager's son, who really doesn't give a toss.

Characters

- Manager
- Co-worker (the manager's son)
- Homeowner or two

Locations

- Manager's office
- Private home

Challenge

There is an initial scene in which the challenger meets the manager's son with whom he or she will be working. The manager is present and the work is explained.

This involves going to a private house, meeting the owner and carrying out the work as per instructions.

The instructions are handed over – these involve preparing and painting a number of rooms. Substitute props will need to be prepared.

The likely pair goes to the house.

They are welcomed in and shown the main room. There are one or two large items in the main room that have to be moved out before painting can commence. (Chairs can be used to represent these.)

The homeowner goes out and the two start work. However, the partner is very casual. He manages to break one of the items and causes other problems such as making marks on the wall. The partner urges that they cover up all these errors.

How does the challenger respond?

Assuming he goes along with the cover-up, the homeowner returns and after some chat, notices the damage. The one who caused the damage denies all knowledge.

If the challenger doesn't go along with the proposal to organise a cover-up, then the partner uses all his authority to threaten him. After all, he's the manager's son. He might well add insult to injury by proposing that they steal a few items to stick it to the homeowner.

Various courses of action are open to the challenger: going along with the denial, taking the blame, telling the truth, or calling up the boss on the phone.

Evaluation

- How did the challenger deal with the problem?
- What course of action was taken and what were the consequences?
- Could a better course of action have been taken?
- What were the good points to note and where were mistakes made?

Cold Turkey

'Has got me on the run…' The focus here is on the meaning of friendship.

Set-Up

The challenge involves dealing with a friend who is coming down off drugs. The challenger has invited this friend to live with him for a few days so he stays out of trouble while trying to kick the habit. The drug itself needs to be an addictive, Class A drug. The ex-user needs to be played by someone who can relate to the situation. There needs to be adequate preparation with the two players – the challenger and the friend – in order that both understand the situation clearly. What's especially important is they understand their characters' relationship.

Characters

- Friend/s

Location

- Living room

Challenge

Essentially, the player who is in role as the ex-user has the task of trying to get out of the room. Once out of the room, drugs can be located via contacts on the street, and purchased. He shouldn't use force but can use trickery as well as emotional blackmail and simple persuasion. The challenger's task is to make the ex-user stay in the flat. There is another friend who can be called on to run errands if necessary.

The ex-user may move on to use pleading, tears, emotional blackmail or the logic of criminal code in order to be allowed out of the room. The challenger's task is to counter these arguments.

Evaluation

- What effective strategies were used by the challenger?
- What ineffective strategies were used?
- What wasn't used at all but might have been?

Negotiation Skills

The following scenarios call for the challenger to demonstrate skills in:

- Diplomacy
- Persuasiveness
- Assertiveness
- Understanding and maintaining priorities

The Job Centre

A variation on 'He was giving me a funny look' *is, of course,* 'He was giving my girlfriend a funny look.' *The focus here is on dealing with multiple tasks simultaneously.*

Set-Up

The challenge relies on having a young woman in the group who is willing to play the part of the challenger's girlfriend.

The setting is a job centre waiting room.

The challenger is going to there to 'sign on', to register as unemployed.

Characters

- Girlfriend
- Male drunk
- Two clerks
- Other applicants (if required)

Location

- Job centre

Challenge

The girlfriend and the challenger go and collect a ticket which gives them a place in the queue. They sit and wait for their number to be called.

A drunk comes in and sits apart from them and starts looking at the girlfriend but not speaking. He might nod or smile.

The task of the woman playing the girlfriend is to stay neutral but not to move away from the man.

Then a clerk goes to his or her position and calls the challenger over.

The clerk will start going through various questions: name, date of birth, address, previous employment, qualifications, etc. (The answers given need to be true to the challenger.) However, the clerk is quite slow and forgetful. He or she occasionally calls over another clerk for assistance.

Meanwhile, the drunk man moves in on the girlfriend. He goes to sit next to her. She shows that she is a little uncomfortable but doesn't actually move away.

It should be evident to the challenger what is going on via his line of sight.

How does the challenger deal with the escalating attentions of the drunk when the girlfriend is clearly not good at dealing with him herself? Does he appeal to the clerk or deal with it himself?

If the challenger goes to deal with the drunk, the clerk might go on lunch or invite another applicant to the desk.

Evaluation

- What impact did the challenger's behaviour or passivity have on the girlfriend?
- What did the decisions of the challenger say about his priority in the situation?
- What was the outcome?
- Was it a good or bad outcome?
- If bad, how could it have been different?

The Burger Bar

There are no labels on hamburgers served over the counter. The focus here is on the assessment of risk.

Set-Up

This is quite an elaborate set-up, mainly because a good few people are needed to take roles.

The challenger is given a job managing a mobile burger bar. Part of the challenge is just dealing with orders from customers. To make this exercise workable, you need a currency – substitutes for money – and something else for burgers, chips and so on. It's worth taking time to prepare these bits and pieces in advance. It's useful also to have various denominations represented: £5, £1, 50p, etc.

The challenger in this role has a boss, who owns the burger bar, and also an assistant. The setting is a small, local festival.

The van is reasonably well supplied for the day, but the problem arises because there are more customers than burgers.

Characters

- Burger-bar owner
- Burger-bar assistant
- Customers
- Health official

Location

- Burger bar in a field where there's a festival on

Challenge

The challenge begins with the owner of the bar explaining to the challenger how to run the bar. The assistant is introduced. Then the owner leaves.

At this point the customers start to arrive and to place orders. The scene needs to be managed so the challenger is under pressure but not overwhelmed.

Let's imagine that an order for burger and chips involves preparing a piece of cardboard inside two pieces of polystyrene (not much different from life, really), along with some paper strips.

The facilitator then moves time forward.

The assistant announces, as per the set-up, that there are no more burgers. It's only early in the afternoon. However, he has a friend who could supply them – he just needs to run over there. It's a choice for the challenger; the provenance of these burgers is not known. However, there's still clearly a market for them out there. If the decision is taken not to get the new burgers in, then the challenger has to deal with complaining customers. The boss also returns and demands to know why the bar isn't running. And getting in more stock is an obvious thing to do.

If the decision is taken to get in the burgers, then time is moved on and we pick up the story as the assistant returns. There's a second dilemma because on the box is clear indication that the burgers are beyond their 'use-by' date.

If the decision is taken to serve them, then time moves forward again enabling one of the customers to return and complain that his or her son has been sick after eating a burger.

A further development can involve this customer calling over a council health officer who is supervising the festival, to explain what has occurred.

Evaluation

- What was the decision made and, also important, what was the decision rejected?
- What was the outcome of this decision?
- Could a better decision have been made?
- What is more important: health and safety or profit with risk?
- Is it more important to stick to your principles and, if necessary, aggravate your employer?

The Post Office

Just when you thought it was safe to buy stamps again… The focus here is on patience, diligence and coping with pressure.

Set-Up

This exercise is a little complex, but if put together well, works like a barbecue roasting chestnuts.

The challenger works in a second-hand car showroom. The job is pretty ordinary and doesn't require any special knowledge. He has a friend who isn't working and is a little resentful that his friend has paid work. On this particular day, the challenger's boss sold a car but omitted to hand over the car manual. So it needs to be sent out to the new owner as soon as possible.

It's the end of the day on Friday.

Characters

- Friend
- Manager of car showroom
- Post Office clerk
- Customers at the Post Office

Locations

- Car showroom
- Manager's office
- Post Office

Challenge

The boss explains to the challenger that the car manual needs to go in the post. He or she hands the challenger the manual along with paper, pen, tape, money for stamps and the address. The manager explains that it needs to go in the post tonight, and to make sure to get a receipt. The boss will be working late so could he bring the receipt back?

This is the first task: to wrap the parcel.

As he's doing this, his friend arrives and wants to go to the pub. The friend's task is to chat to the challenger and persuade him to forget the task until Monday.

Then the challenger needs to take the parcel to the Post Office. There's a queue in there, which gives the friend further ammunition to argue for jacking in the task. The person at the head of the queue takes a long time submitting forms.

The challenger reaches the head of the queue. If there is any problem with the wrapping or the addressing of the parcel, then the clerk must ask for the problem to be sorted out before it's accepted for posting. The player playing the Post Office clerk has full licence to be picky.

Finally, the challenger needs to take the receipt back to the showroom.

Evaluation

- Did the challenger manage to keep his temper throughout?

- Was the friend dealt with well or badly?

- Did the challenger complete all the stages of the task?

- Which stages were missed, and why?

Drugs in Prison

A role play for a prison context. The focus here is on awareness and maintenance of personal priorities.

Set-Up

This scenario was devised for young offenders about to be transferred to an adult prison. It's important that players in the group are familiar with prison culture.

The background is that the challenger is about to be placed in a cell with an inmate who is dealing drugs.

To make matters more complicated, another prisoner also has access to drugs in that building.

During the challenge, the challenger will experience several encounters; all give him an opportunity to use his communication and negotiation skills to keep himself out of trouble.

Characters

- Prison officer/s
- Cellmate
- Another two prisoners

Locations

- Prison cell and corridor
- Officer's office

Challenge

The challenge begins with the officer bringing in the newcomer (the challenger) to his cell. It's a meeting with his new cellmate. The officer leaves. Another prisoner comes to the door, finds the dealer not alone, and so calls him out for a conversation.

In the conversation, which the newcomer can overhear, the dealer is told that some drugs have been arranged to be thrown over the wall in a day or so. When the dealer returns to his cell, he's concerned that the newcomer may have overheard the conversation. He questions the newcomer.

Time moves on to 'association', when prisoners are allowed to circulate in the recreation area.

During association, another prisoner comes up to the newcomer to warn him about his cellmate. This new prisoner says he will give him protection if he wants. There's an intimation that this prisoner is also dealing.

When the newcomer returns to his cell, his cellmate is in there, angry that apparently some drugs have been taken from the cell. He accuses the newcomer of taking them.

The noise alerts the officer who calls by and tells the newcomer to come to the wing office.

In the office, the officer asks how the newcomer is getting on. The officer suggests it would be useful if the newcomer could report anything in the way of evident rule-breaking.

(It's also possible to bring the second prisoner who gave warnings to the newcomer into the room during the conversation and have him simply sit down and listen. This opens up the possibility that (a) the officer is corrupt, or (b) the prisoner is in collusion with the officer, or (c) both.)

How does the challenger deal with this situation? It may not be as easy as deciding to cooperate with the authority in the situation if it's apparent that the officer is colluding himself with drug-dealing.

When the newcomer returns to his cell, his cellmate might apologise for his former accusation (he mislaid his own drugs) and possibly question him about the visit to the wing office.

Evaluation

The challenger has had a sequence of problematic interactions to negotiate: with the cellmate, with the officer and with the other prisoner.

- Did the challenger manage to stay out of trouble?

- What decision was made about either conspiring with his cellmate or telling on him to the prison officer?

- If the challenger told the prison officer about the drug-dealing, what effect did this have on the newcomer's position amongst the inmates?

- Should one stick to one's principles despite the consequences?

The Mobile Phone Shop

The predicament of being thrust into a conflict not of your own making. The focus here is on managing conflicting truths.

Set-Up

The challenger has a friend who runs a mobile phone shop. Unbeknownst to him on this particular day, his friend is going to phone him up and ask him to run the shop for the day. (The challenge works best if the challenger really does know a little about the phone business.) This has happened before once or twice so the challenger knows roughly how it goes. On this occasion, however, he will be on his own.

As in other challenges, paper money needs be created and some dummy phones.

Characters

- Friend, the manager
- Two or three customers each with a different task

Locations

- Domestic environment
- Mobile phone shop

Challenge

The challenger starts at home where he receives the call from his friend, the shop manager. Coming into the shop, the manager explains that he has an urgent family issue to deal with and he needs to be away for a couple of hours.

Assuming the challenger accepts the task of running the shop, the first customer comes in and, looking shifty, asks to look at several phones. This might be a thief who'll take advantage if an opportunity arises.

The second person comes in, looking angry, and says that she's come to be paid. She says she was working there temporarily and hasn't yet been paid by the owner. She evidently knows both the manager and the shop so may well be genuine. She has an invoice with her.

The third person to arrive is a man with a box of twenty phones, which he claims he delivers regularly for cash. Again, he appears to know the manager and how the shop functions. He asks for £200 in cash and he has the paperwork.

The manager can't be reached on the phone during any of these encounters.

Evaluation

- How did the challenger deal with the various problems?

- How was a balance found between serving the interests of the shop, and serving the interests of the customers?

- Was there any evidence of creative thinking in the way the problems were tackled?

- How did those in the group who were playing the customers feel about how they were dealt with?

Assertiveness

The following scenarios call for the challenger to demonstrate skills in:

- Communicating a point of view
- Managing relationships
- Holding to a principle

CHALLENGES – Assertiveness

Carpets by Moonlight

How to keep your head when those around you are sticking theirs into holes in the ground. The focus here is on holding to principle.

Set-Up

The situation is that of a small carpet company that does sales and fittings. For a while now the company hasn't been doing too well, so the workers have got together, unbeknownst to the management, and have been moonlighting – selling stock door to door, fitting it straight away and pocketing the money. They generally do this at weekends.

This is the context into which the challenger arrives as a new member of the team. He replaces someone that's just left, who was very much involved in the moonlighting.

Characters

- Boss
- Four or five workers
- Homeowners (if required)

Locations

- Carpet shop office
- Carpet shop backroom
- Street
- Front door

Challenge

The challenger meets the manager who explains the work: he is to become part of the team and go out with the others when required.

Then he's taken to meet the team. The manager goes. Since it's a Friday, the conversation is turning to the weekend. The team confidentially explain what happens some weekends. They take the van and go moonlighting. *'The money is pretty good.'*

The challenger has a choice – to go along or not.

1) If the challenger refuses to go along with the group, time moves forward to Monday when

they all arrive back, talking of the money they made and how they spent it. They also give the cold shoulder to the newcomer, making it clear he's not one of the group.

The manager calls the newcomer into the backroom. Does he know anything about stock going missing? If the challenger tells the truth about what's happening, the manager should then sack the moonlighters. At the end of the day, they are waiting to confront the challenger at the end of the street… If he conceals the truth, the team ostracise him because they *assume* he has told the truth.

2) If the challenger goes along with the moonlighting, a scene can be run in the van where the team is driving along, probably smoking pot, and moaning about the company. They might drive up outside a house, making the newcomer be the one who goes to the door.

Then time moves on and we go to Monday. The group is together again in the backroom. The manager comes in and addresses the group. He says that the company van was seen in the vicinity of this particular estate, and does anyone know anything? He has in his hand a description of the individuals seen, and curiously one of the descriptions matches that of the challenger…

As with all these exercises, a certain amount of improvisation is required both in the playing and (re-)structuring of the scenes. In this second scenario, for example, if the entire team gets the sack, then the story might be extended by someone in the group suggesting to the challenger they come back that night and burn down the shop.

Evaluation

- How did the challenger deal with the peer pressure?
- Did the challenger use good communication skills?
- Was help asked for at any point?
- What kind of trouble did the challenger get into?
- Might this have been avoided?

Bullying at Work

Is this bullying or am I imagining it? And if it is, does anyone really care? The focus here is on diplomacy.

Set-Up

The challenger is starting a new job in a warehouse. He is coming into a work context where there's bullying going on. In the set-up, the relationship between the two principle characters, the bully and the bullied, needs to be clearly defined.

Characters

* Manager
* Co-worker

Location

* Warehouse area

Challenge

The challenger is sent down to a section of the warehouse where he is to work with a colleague.

He meets the colleague who is quiet and soft-spoken. The colleague explains what they have to do when a load arrives.

Then the manager arrives to check the newcomer is settling in. Almost straight away the manager refers to the co-worker in a dismissive and patronising way. There are one or two jokes made at his expense, possibly drawing attention to skin or hair colour, height or weight. The bullied co-worker joins in the jokes weakly and makes no complaint about the bullying behaviour.

Then the manager goes.

There is an opportunity here for the challenger to raise the issue of apparent bullying. Does he take it?

The co-worker replies by merely stating that this is how it goes. And since there is no work on, would the challenger like to smoke a spliff around the back?

If the challenger agrees, then round the back the co-worker explains about how he is lucky to have the job anyway, given his previous prison record and the fact he told a few lies on his application form.

If the challenger refuses the offer, the co-worker goes by himself and the manager returns. The manager starts apologising for the co-worker's ineptitude, explaining that the challenger might as well be working alone for all the difference his co-worker makes. Does the challenger intervene?

Then the co-worker returns. The manager immediately accuses him of using drugs on the premises, giving him a further opportunity to criticise and bully him. But he doesn't sack him. That would take away the bully's fun.

Evaluation

- How does the challenger deal with the bullying?
- What kinds of tactics are used and which are successful?
- If there is a confrontation with the manager, does the challenger manage to keep the co-worker onside?
- Are there any tactics that might have been used more successfully?

Taking Care of Grandpa

When the old become objects of fun for the young. The focus here is on looking after family.

Set-Up

The challenger is asked to imagine he has an old grandfather or perhaps a more distant relative. This individual is getting old and is less and less able to be self-determined – and so needs help.

The challenger is asked to go round and help him. It has happened before. The challenger is also told that he has a good friend who's not always very responsible.

Characters

- Grandfather
- Friend
- Family member (if required)

Location

- Grandfather's house

Challenge

On stage first is the old relative, pottering about in his room. He's clearly absent-minded and a little confused. The challenger arrives and is welcomed in. The old relative has various awkward tasks for the challenger. These might involve reading the newspaper out loud to him, moving furniture around, and so on. There is also money lying around and in his absent-minded way, the relative sometimes tries to press it on his grandchild. There may also be personal items such as war medals out on show.

During this, the friend arrives, having been told by the challenger's family that this is where his mate has gone. The role of the friend is really to raise the stakes of the challenge by taking a dismissive attitude towards the grandparent. This might involve making jokes at his expense, teasing him, bullying him or taking money off the table.

The challenger clearly has a responsibility of care towards the elderly relative. At the same time, to lose a friend would not be a good outcome.

One way for the scenario to develop is for another relative to arrive who knows the grandparent well. He or she might discover that some money is missing, and bring one or both of the visitors to account.

Evaluation

- How well did the challenger manage to establish a relationship with the grandfather?
- How did the challenger deal with the intervention of the friend?
- How did the challenger balance competing priorities – to look after the relative and maintain his friendship?

The Fire Station

Another role play in which the challenger is cast as a newcomer and the rituals of the natives take a little getting used to. The focus here is on diplomacy.

Set-Up

There's a group of firefighters in a fire station. Today they are going to welcome a new recruit.

The distinctive aspect of this group of firefighters is that they have a particular ritual or game that they like to enact whenever a newcomer arrives. It's something of an initiation ceremony.

The station also has a supervisor who may or may not approve of what goes on.

The group need to work out – while the challenger is out of the room – just what this ritual or game involves. It needs to be something in which all participate, not simply an excuse to bully the newcomer. The aim is to create an event that is a little embarrassing and confusing to participate in, rather than anything involving violence, nakedness or humiliation (so obviously it's only partly based on reality). Maybe it's a game played without shoes or one involving blindfolds or balloons – or all of these.

Characters

- Supervisor of the team
- Team of firefighters

Locations

- Staff area
- Supervisor's office

Challenge

The first scene is a meeting with the supervisor in which the challenger is welcomed. Then the challenger is introduced to the firefighting team and the supervisor retires.

Now is the time for the initiation.

If the challenger goes along with it, the supervisor might come back when, for example, the challenger is blindfolded. The supervisor might very well turn out to be shocked by what is taking place, and keen to learn why the newcomer agreed to participate. Is this the correct attitude when you might at any moment be called on to save lives?

Alternatively, if the challenger declines to participate, then one of the team can go and report this to the supervisor who will bring the challenger in and explain to him that this is the way things go in this fire station.

Evaluation

- How did the challenger respond to the invitation to the initiation?
- What were his internal thoughts at that time?
- How did he find the experience of being made a fool of?
- Could he have, on reflection, handled the situation better?

CHALLENGES – Assertiveness

Talking to the School

Conceptually simple, hard to execute. The focus here is on honesty.

Set-Up

The purpose of the exercise is to test the challenger to speak openly about his previous life. It works best for those who have a personal history involving drugs, alcohol or crime.

He has been asked to give a talk to a class in a secondary school.

He is required to talk about his own life to date, and about mistakes made that are now regretted.

The rest of the group need to be primed not to play up during the challenge.

Characters

- Teacher
- Pupils in a secondary school

Location

- Classroom

Challenge

The challenger gives the talk – which can be prepared a little in advance – and takes questions from the audience.

Evaluation

- Was the speaker candid? Assertive? Clear?
- Did the speaker create a good relationship with the pupils?
- Did the speaker ask for clarity over any issue from the teacher? (This might have meant questions about swearing or giving details of drugs use, etc.)
- Did the audience learn anything from the talk?

Managing Emotions

The following scenarios call for the challenger to demonstrate skills in:

- Controlling anger
- Avoiding impulsive behaviour
- Patience
- Careful use of language
- Reasoning skills

The Broken Radio

There's nothing the indecisive find more difficult than a pincer movement. The focus here is on knowing what's worth fighting for.

Set-Up

This challenge was created for a prison setting. The backstory is that character A has loaned a radio to character B. Character A also has a friend, character C. But B and C don't like each other much. Let's call these characters Ade, Benny and Charlie.

If the genders are mixed, it will alter the dynamic a little.

The challenger is going to be taking the role of Ade, who has loaned the radio. And as far as he knows, and he should know, the radio was working when it was loaned.

Characters

- Ade
- Benny
- Charlie
- Prison officer (if required)

Location

- Recreation area in a prison

Challenge

Ade is chatting with Charlie when Benny brings the radio back. It could also be a CD or a DVD; the important point is, the thing is broken or doesn't work when returned. Benny maintains that it was already broken when he borrowed it.

If the challenger accepts his word on this, then when Benny has gone, Charlie starts working on the challenger, arguing that he knows for a fact Benny is lying because he, Charlie, heard Benny playing the thing only yesterday. And Ade is really being taken for a mug here. This is the point of the challenge – the actor playing Charlie is trying to wind up the challenger emotionally. The challenger's task is to stay calm and keep things in perspective.

Charlie might even call Benny back in order to take him on directly. The player playing Benny might then respond to this and become aggressive himself.

The scenario has the potential for escalation, especially if a prison officer appears and completely misunderstands what's going on.

How does the challenger resolve the conflict? Charlie is clearly using the situation to maintain his own war with Benny. For the challenger, it's a question of keeping his own emotions under control while listening to the other parties, finding a line to take in the situation, and asserting himself. After all, in the final analysis, it is his radio.

Evaluation

- Did the challenger keep his emotions under control?

- Was he able to stay friends with both Benny and Charlie in the scene?

- Did he get manipulated by either Benny or Charlie?

- What were his thoughts and feelings throughout?

112

CHALLENGES – Managing Emotions

The Adult Education Class

When the cat's away, the rat comes along and chews the mouse's head off. The focus here is on being patient and keeping calm.

Set-Up

It's an adult education evening class but today there are only two pupils. The subject matter needs to be something the facilitator is comfortable teaching, so reading/writing/comprehension is always a good way to go.

The challenger is going to play the first pupil.

This exercise is about provoking the challenger. It's about testing that individual's ability to cope with teasing and aggravation.

The role of the provoking pupil is a key one, so needs to be played by one of the facilitators or a group member who can pitch the provocation at just the right level.

Characters

- Teacher
- Another pupil
- Other pupils (if required)

Location

- Classroom

Challenge

At the beginning, the disruptive pupil is already in the space with some study materials. The teacher brings in the challenger and there are introductions. The teacher then starts to teach, setting out a task that needs to be done while the teacher is out of the room. This might be, for example, to précis an article in a newspaper, or to rewrite the article from another point of view.

Once the teacher has left the room, the disruptive pupil can start trying to get the attention of the other pupil. This might involve flicking bits of paper, moving around the room or talking. The task of the person playing this role is to trigger an emotional response. The task of the challenger is to manage

166

any emotions he feels in the situation, and to avoid argument.

The disruptive pupil might:

- Comment on the other pupil's reading ability
- Talk about 'fancying the teacher'
- Try to copy what the other is writing
- Pretend to be illiterate
- Flirt with the other pupil

At some point the teacher will return. At this point, the disruptive pupil can make up stories about the challenger. (One justification for this behaviour might be that the disruptive pupil lacks any confidence in reading or writing and picks on the other one to detract attention from this fact.) It's very possible that on returning to the classroom, the teacher will take the side of the disruptive pupil, in order to keep the pressure on the challenger.

There's always the option of bringing in other pupils who are friends of the disruptive pupil.

Evaluation

- Did the challenger become emotionally engaged? It's not the case that he 'shouldn't' – it's pretty inevitable that this will happen – it's more a case of acknowledging when it does happen and then looking at the management of the challenger's responses.
- How did the challenger deal with the other pupil?
- How did the challenger deal with the teacher?
- Did the challenger feel at any point like either punching one of them or walking out?

The Bully Boyfriend

When a simple task turns into something a lot more complicated. The focus here is on the perils of being a rescuer.

Set-Up

This challenge is for a young man, but could be used for a young woman with some alteration. The backstory is that the young man has been asked by his girlfriend, who is in hospital, to get something for her from the family home, where she still lives. Probably it's something like books or a CD.

When he goes round there, he's going to find that his girlfriend's sister is being bullied by her boyfriend.

Characters

- Girlfriend's sister
- Her boyfriend
- Other family members (if required)
- Girlfriend on the phone (if required)

Location

- Girlfriend's house, living room

Challenge

The challenger knocks at the door and is invited in by his girlfriend's sister. Let's call this character Emilia. At this point there's no one else in the room, although her boyfriend Pete is upstairs. Emilia engages the challenger in conversation. She asks about her sister. However, she behaves in a way to show clearly that she's upset. The challenger is likely to ask her what's wrong. If he doesn't, she should tell him. The fact is, she's being bullied by her boyfriend. He's started to be violent towards her; nothing too serious, but it's very upsetting. *'Do you think you could help at all?'* she asks.

Soon after, Pete comes downstairs. He asks why the challenger is here and then starts mocking him for being an errand boy for his girlfriend. The boyfriend also openly teases and runs Emilia down, making disparaging comments about her.

How does the challenger deal with this situation? The aim is to avoid becoming overly involved on an emotional level to the point where he might respond aggressively. Instead, he should try to help the sister as best he can.

Evaluation

- To what extent did the challenger feel obliged to intervene?
- What tactics did he use with the boyfriend?
- Were they effective?
- Where there other strategies that might have been tried, but weren't?
- To what extent did the challenger feel this was his business?

Zone of Confrontation

Practising an encounter that is feared may make the encounter in reality easier to manage – not because the player is necessarily better equipped, but because he or she feels more equipped. The focus here is on courage.

Set-Up

This exercise was devised specifically for a young man who was fearful about leaving prison. He was worried about former enemies coming after him. He was understandably vague about exactly what had happened in the past, but he did believe that there were people waiting for him on the outside, with revenge in mind. Given these circumstances, it was almost inevitable, he thought, that he would be obliged to use violence against them in order to defend himself. He believed that he was incapable of *not* using violence in that situation. The aim of the challenge then became to change his belief in this inevitability and to give him a sense that he could deal with any provocation non-violently.

We established a zone on the floor of the room, which was marked out with chalk. He had to remain in that zone whatever happened, and to deal with anything that happened there without resorting to violence. While he was out of the room, a number of provocations were planned. Most of these would use inference rather than detailed accusation. (Besides, we didn't know the story of his offence or anything of its legacy.)

Characters

- Various undefined provocateurs

Location

- Circle or rectangle drawn in chalk on the floor, large enough for three or four people to walk around in

Challenge

Intermittently, individuals would enter the zone and confront the challenger. The comments made to him would be along the lines of:

- *'So you're back then?'*
- *'So you ready for what's coming?'*
- *'If I was you, I wouldn't hang around here, mate.'*

The aim of the provocateurs is to rile the challenger, to make him angry, to make him lose his cool. The challenger's task is to stay calm and communicate on a friendly level.

The level of provocations can be raised as time goes on, with pairs of hostile provocateurs coming in. The challenger's personal space can be closed down and more direct challenges to him can be made – about his cowardice, his guilt over what happened or about his fear.

Evaluation

- What were the thoughts and feelings the challenger had while the challenge was progressing?
- Were there thoughts and feelings that he didn't act on?
- How comfortable or uncomfortable did he feel?
- How did his actual ability to cope compare with what he anticipated would be his inability?
- Did the experience of doing the challenge change his anticipation of how he might cope with what happens when he's released from prison?

Mistaken Identity

What it's like to go somewhere where everyone knows your name – only it's not your name. The focus here is on reasoning skills.

Set-Up

The set-up is simple: there are two or three scenes in which the challenger is treated by strangers as someone he isn't. He's not told in advance this is going to happen. The players need to be very clear about who they think he is and what that person did that earned their disapproval.

The settings might be a nightclub (exterior) and pub (interior).

Characters

- Bouncer
- Friend
- Barman
- Strangers
- Young girl (if required)

Locations

- Outside a nightclub
- Pub

Challenge

The challenger and a friend, either male or female, meet up to go to a nightclub. When they arrive, the bouncer doesn't let them in. Initially, he doesn't give a reason and when the friend asks, the bouncer says *'You know the reason. It's your mate. He's not allowed. You can come in but not him.'* The friend insists they stick together so suggests they go to a pub instead.

They go into a pub and the barman says *'Only one drink and then you're out.'* Essentially, it's the same story. *'It's because of your mate there.'* But the barman, like the bouncer, doesn't give any explanation.

Sitting down, the friend asks the challenger: *'Have you done anything you should be ashamed of? What have you done to make people behave like this?'*

Soon after, a stranger enters the pub and goes immediately up to the challenger. He says something like *'You've got a nerve coming in here. Right – outside.'*

It's important that the players know the backstory: that the challenger is the spitting image of a trouble-maker in the area who has caused fights in several pubs and clubs, in part because of a volatile relationship with an under-age girl. These facts can be referred to, as and when it's useful.

The task for the challenger is to remain calm and use reasoning skills to avoid physical conflict. The player playing the friend can be more or less supportive in order to keep up the level of challenge. If he or she should start to withdraw the friendship, especially in the middle of a fracas, this will tend to make it somewhat more precarious for the challenger.

Evaluation

- How did the challenger feel when strangers started recognising him?
- Did he consider using violence at any point to assert himself?
- Did he stay calm and keep aggression out of his voice?
- How did he resolve the situation?
- Might there have been a better way?

PART SIX

TRAINING

I developed these exercises to help group leaders
and facilitators working with difficult groups, to
acquaint themselves with the challenges involved.
It's important to understand these are training
exercises and not to be used like other exercises in
the book, i.e. with the groups themselves.

Pushing

This is a series of exercises that were developed out of a simple physicalisation of effort in conflict, fashioned by Augusto Boal within his Theatre of the Oppressed. They pivot around the idea of resistance, and coping positively with it. The core exercise functions as a kind of metaphor for the relationship between the facilitator and the individual or group offering resistance. Most of the time players will operate in pairs during the sequence. In each pair, one player is effectively playing the role of the facilitator while the other is playing the role of the individual who is either resisting engagement with the project or demonstrating negative or destructive behaviour. So the person playing this latter role is rather like a boxing or football coach creating problems that simulate the behaviour of the opposition. It's important to be aware; that it's a training situation not a competitive one, and the degree of difficult behaviour needs be measured out appropriately. The player in the role of the facilitator is to deal with the resistance presented, by creating inventive and varied strategies that have the end result of both absorbing the oppositional energy and incorporating it into play.

Stage One

The group is divided into pairs. It's useful if the two players in each pair are not too dissimilar in weight and height.

The two players in each pair find a light physical contact using the tips of fingers, and then walk around the room.

Then one player consciously leads the other, maintaining just a light finger-to-finger contact. This arrangement can be swapped over after a while.

Then the two players stand facing each other and each places a palm against the opposite palm. So player A's left hand is against player B's right, and so on. They then push against each other, initially without moving off the spot. This section is about getting used to handling physical pressure and moderating one's own energy to meet it (but not defeat it).

Then the players move off the spot, keeping palm-to-palm contact and pushing each other around the room. The aim is to be playful; both pushing and allowing oneself to be pushed.

As the exercise goes on, the pushing can become more active and energetic – still avoiding competitiveness. The focus of each player needs to be on feeling the energy of the other person, and meeting it. As it changes in intensity, the player needs to push harder or less hard in order to maintain the dramatic play between them; a play which is achieved through the maintenance of a certain physical tension.

Stage Two

Next, one player takes a different role: he or she becomes an obstacle, almost a deadweight. The other player has to move this player around the room using physical means. The obstacle player can simply stand immobile, lie on the floor or sit – whatever he or she does, the other has to find a strategy that will succeed: pulling, lifting, shifting or carrying. Initially, the obstacle player shouldn't be too unhelpful, otherwise it can have the effect of defeating the other player. However, as time goes on, the deadweight can legitimately become a little awkward.

There's a principle here: when the obstacle player senses that the moving player has solved the problem (of getting the two of them around the room), then he or she changes weight or position, so the successful stratagem ceases to be effective. Now, the moving player has to come up with a new idea because the old one doesn't work. After a while, the two can swap roles.

Then all the pairs go down one end of the room. The aim now is for one player in each pair to move their obstacle partner down to the other end of the room (and maybe back again depending on the size of the room). It's essentially the same exercise as they were running previously, only now there is a track and a destination. The obstacle player continues to make things difficult for his or her partner. However, the obstacle player must eventually always allow the other to achieve the objective of getting them both to the end of the room. This is important, both to prevent competitiveness taking over and to ensure that the facilitating player doesn't give up, jeopardising the positive dynamic between them. Once the moving player has brought the obstacle player across the room, then the two swap roles.

Assuming the room is wide enough, all the players in the room should go at the same time; or if this means the area becoming too crowded, then perhaps in two smaller groups.

Stage Three

This stage involves the pair making the same journey, only with a difference. This time, the moving player should use a mixture of purely physical but also psychological and emotional means to get the other across the room. This means using words – verbal encouragements – and it means the player playing the obstacle can respond in the same way, taking the resistance role into language. So it's a kind of game between them, one pushing but now also encouraging, complementing, enthusing or joking with the other player to get him or her across. In turn, the resisting player starts to express boredom, disquiet, resentment or irritation at being coerced across the room – while still maintaining an element of physical resistance. However, the play between them needs to remain relatively abstract; it shouldn't become 'a scene' between a mother and child or a fight between a teacher and a pupil. Such an extrapolation into a different terrain of drama tends to permit an avoidance of dealing with the resistance in the here and now. For the same reason, there shouldn't be bribes offered that can't be delivered – a strategy that would only create a false reality on top of the one we're working with.

So there should be a balance created between physical and verbal means in the bringing of the other player across the room. Then, as before, the two swap roles. Again, all the pairs can be travelling together.

Stage Four

The third time the pairs cross the space, there is no physical contact allowed at all. It all has to be entirely verbal. Both the resisting person and the coaxing person have equally to use non-contact means. So the reluctant player is all '*Why should I?*' and '*I can't be bothered.*' There's a fair bit of '*This is all shit*' and '*Can we have a break now?*' Whereas the coaxing player has to use positive incitements. Again, bribes are disallowed. It's no good promising a pint of beer if it can't actually be delivered. Nor should the exercise turn into a scene. The exercise has to remain in the abstract, without definition. However, there are still many ways to play '*Come over to the other side of this room*', simply using humour, inventiveness, observation, intelligence and playfulness. The exercise can be taxing for the facilitator, but that's the intention. In the experience of being taxed, the player can discover facilitative strategies in this relatively risk-free environment that might otherwise, in more stressful contexts, not be risked. The relationship between the two players is a much bigger imaginative space than is sometimes imagined, with many potential interactive dances available. This tends to become apparent in the feedback.

As part of the exercise, it's useful to suggest that if words or phrases are said by the facilitator that the other player doesn't like, then the obstacle player should show this by walking backwards instead of forwards. This clearly signals to the facilitator that he or she is using a strategy that's alienating the other player. The facilitating player knows to reframe the request or try something completely different.

When running the exercise, I've encouraged participants, as they play, to note what works well and what doesn't, and to remember these observations for the feedback session. I'm also interested to know what spoken or physical behaviours by the resisting player cause the facilitating player to become angry or want to throw in the towel. These hot spots can be made an interesting focus for discussion later.

Stage Five

After this last section has been run and all the players have experienced both roles, it'll be time for some reflection on what occurred. It's good to ask not only about what worked and what didn't but how the person playing the obstacle felt playing that role. Did they get any insight into what the facilitator should be contributing? It's often the case that these kinds of observations come forward:

- *'I liked it when she took the pressure off me.'*
- *'I liked it when she made it a journey that we were both going to make.'*
- *'I liked it when it became more about play and less about obligation.'*
- *'I liked it when she was honest about why she was running this project.'*
- *'I liked it when she acknowledged her own mistakes.'*

Hopefully, we'll emerge with something of a picture of the most effective strategies – incorporating both verbal and behavioural strategies – that work to dynamise and engage a group of no-sayers.

There's also a discussion to be had around the facilitator's thoughts and feelings during the exercise. How did he or she feel when presented with this resistant behaviour? Was there anything said or displayed that was particularly riling or even completely disempowering? Was it a surprise to find oneself a recipient of these feelings? Are there any useful reflections coming out of this about personal values or shared, perhaps false, assumptions of how antisocial young people behave?

Stage Six

Now the pairs are broken up and we have one large group. This group can then be divided into two subgroups with a larger one and a smaller one. The larger should be around twice the size of the smaller. So perhaps five players and ten players in the two groups. Keeping to the same principles used for the earlier part of the exercise, this time the smaller group are going to facilitate the first part of a session for the larger group.

The larger group is asked to take the roles of disaffected young people and to spread out around the room. These players are free to do what they like: chat, make phone calls, lie around, read or whatever. The small group's task is to bring everyone together so that they end up sitting on the chairs in a circle. The exercise represents a kind of prologue to what will be the first act.

An assumption needs to be made about the age group of the participants and the imagined structure of the planned 'session'. For example, these are thirteen- to fifteen-year-olds brought together for the first of a series of workshops that will involve creating a performance on the theme of turf wars or the likelihood of aliens. In private, those playing the young people might additionally decide who amongst them are the acknowledged leaders, those who tend to make waves.

The members of the smaller group need to collaborate to plan and execute a strategy. Will they have a leader, a spokesperson? Will they split up and talk to the young people individually or address them as one group? Will there be any prearranged means of communication between them during the exercise?

As before, they will meet resistance. But also as before, the larger group are under strict instructions to acquiesce in creating that circle of chairs *at some point*. However, on the way, they are free to present a range of difficult behaviours to test the facilitators.

The exercise might happily run for thirty minutes or so. The dynamics in the room can become quite complex. If the young people who cooperate early in the exercise and go to sit on chairs aren't looked after while they're there, they may well return to the corners of the room and be far more difficult to eke out a second time.

Individual successes or failures with different young people can have ripples far beyond the personal spaces of those concerned (the facilitators don't necessarily know which of the young people have the most influence).

Evaluation

- Did the small group have a plan and did they execute it?

- Were they drawn away from their plan at all, and if so, how and why?

- What happened unexpectedly to make the plan difficult to carry out?

- If the plan was abandoned, was that done by collective agreement or did it just slowly get ditched?

- Was it any different dealing with a group rather than with individuals?

- If so, what was the difference?

- Who amongst the small group was particularly successful in bringing the others to the chairs and what kind of tactics did they use?

- Were there any key moments that swung the momentum one way or the other?

Brilliant / Shit

This training exercise is about how to deal with participants who, when they get involved in creative practice, can't leave aside their judgement. These are the young people who are often heard delivering comments in the style of a rapid-arms-fire assault on an enemy. Such-and-such piece of work is either '*brilliant*' or '*shit*'. It's '*a load of bollocks*' or occasionally '*brilliant/magic/wicked/amazing/well bad*'. There's no middle ground.

How do you create a dialogue within the space that lies between these two extremes of judgement? It's particularly difficult when you experience the aggression not just from one individual but from the entire group, all reinforcing each other in their sneering condemnation of a particular piece of creative work. To stand up against it feels like you're betraying the group in some way. It's as if by rejecting their verdict you're either admitting to being stupid – because you can't see what they see – or you're determined to make *them* look stupid by arguing that they're wrong. Underlying these feelings is possibly an anxiety about losing the group's willingness to follow your lead in the project as a whole.

Taking a third position between the extremes of '*brilliant*' and '*shit*' is not, of course, about arguing that the group is right or wrong; rather, it's about asserting there are other ways to assess the piece of work. It's also about vocabulary; introducing a conceptual shift in thinking that relies on giving increased value to unfamiliar or previously disparaged terms. The aim is to get the participants thinking differently about creative practice; seeing it as process as well as product, as continuous experiment and discovery rather than simply success and failure, and about merit sitting equally alongside deficiency within the same piece of work.

Preparation

Divide the group into teams of three players. In each team someone will take the role of the facilitator, someone the role of a difficult young person and someone will be an observer. Make sure to determine the age of the young people, perhaps eight to ten years old.

Ask all the young people to take a large – preferably A3 or A2 – piece of paper and some coloured pens and go to a place on their own. Then ask them to draw a picture quickly. It can have any content or subject; the choice is theirs – only it has to be done quickly.

Then take all the facilitators out of the room and give them their instructions out of earshot of the rest. Their task is to get the young people to take an interest in – and get more involved in – the visual arts. They can do this any way they like, but a good starting point is obviously the picture that the young person has made. Explain that it's not necessary to have a visual-arts background for this exercise; common sense and a general arts background will suffice.

Then take the young people out of the space and speak to them together. They have a very different task. Each one is to try and get his or her facilitator to agree that the picture that has been drawn is brilliant. They should allow some time for this. If this objective is achieved, the young person is to take the picture and walk around the room with it, showing it off to others and telling everyone that the facilitator has said that it's brilliant.

If this can't be achieved, if the affirmation of brilliance doesn't come, the player in role as the young person should switch to getting the facilitator to agree that it's shit. If this is achieved, sulk and start to withdraw from the process. Tearing up the picture is an option.

Then ask the observers to come out and ask them to simply to take note of what occurs. Written notes are particularly useful. It's important for the observers to remain outside the action (and this should be said to everyone in the room); the observers are, in effect, invisible. Their task is simply to note down what works for the facilitator and what doesn't.

Exercise

It tends to happen that different teams will generate different outcomes. In one, the facilitator will keep good order and hold the attention of the young person. In another, the young person is bored and listless, perhaps withdrawing from the process. In another, it's not long before the young person is on their feet, parading the picture. Hopefully the observer is noting down the triggers to these different behaviours. They may be caused by the attitude of the facilitator, his or her language, tactics or even body language (where and how you sit is always important).

It's likely that at least one young person will get up and walk the room, interrupting the other groups. Inevitably this takes the facilitators by surprise, so they have an unanticipated random element to deal with. You'll probably notice that some just ignore the interruption and hope it goes away, others engage with the peripatetic young person and others again speak to the facilitator who is attached to that young person. It may be that the facilitator in question has remained at 'base', hoping the young person doesn't cause too much disruption, or else is actually walking around with them, minimising damage.

In terms of the facilitator running the exercise as a whole, it's good to keep out of the action for the most part, merely jumping in to clear up confusions or beat down fires.

Evaluation

It's good to hear first from one of the observers and get a report, before turning to the others in that team to find out if what was perceived from an objective standpoint can be confirmed from a subjective one.

- Did the facilitator recognise when he or she was being effective?
- How did the young person feel at the different points in the session?
- Did it feel good to win?
- What worked for the young person in terms of non-judgemental engagement?

Following the first group, the same process can be followed with the second. What's important is to identify and maybe write up the effective tactics.

I've seen a range of interesting and effective tactics used by facilitators during this exercise. These have included:

- Talking about this being just one picture amongst many that the young person might create.

- Noting how the drawing has connections with paintings or drawings by famous artists either in terms of content or in terms of technical decisions (probably not in terms of technique itself…).

- The facilitator creating a picture of him or herself.

- Getting the young person to add or alter the existing picture.

- Getting the young person to do a new picture incorporating the best elements of the first.

- Getting the young person to see the picture as actually just a fragment of a larger picture – then to create that larger picture, using the fragment.

Once all the teams have contributed, there should be – perhaps written down on a large piece of paper in the centre of the group – a summary of those tactics that were most effective in the exercise.

A New National Flag

This training exercise is about dealing with individuals who all have very different attitudes towards whatever project is being run. One might be wildly enthusiastic, the next sullen and disinterested. It isn't always the case that the first is easier to manage than the second. Often you simply don't know why such-and-such a person is behaving the way they are, but still you have to deal with that behaviour as best you can.

A situation is set up in which some group members are 'programmed' to behave in certain ways within the simulation. The facilitator in each team won't know how each participant is programmed. The programming – giving of precise roles with accompanying behaviours – needs therefore to take place out of earshot of those playing the facilitators.

Preparation

Divide the group into teams of five (or six if you want an observer attached to each group), with four young people and one facilitator within each team. Establish clearly what the ages of the young people will be. I would suggest eleven to thirteen years old.

Take the facilitators outside and explain the task: to get the young people in their team to design an alternative to the national flag. Explain that the government has finally recognised the Union Jack is no longer appropriate for our multicultural times. There's a national competition being run to find a replacement and anyone can enter. That's the basis for the task today. There will be thirty minutes for the task and the aim is for each team to complete one – or several – submissions for the competition. There's also a 'time-out' option available – if the facilitator feels that he or she is losing control over the team, the exercise for that team can be suspended for a few minutes to allow reflection. If it's suspended, then those playing the young people simply come out of role and wait for the resumption. (This also represents an opportunity for the facilitator of the exercise overall to rebrief the young people in that team, perhaps modifying their level of acted antagonism or disinterest.)

Take the young people outside and give them their roles. In each team there might be, for example:

- One quiet introspective young person who is having problems at home.

- One noisy person who is trying to become teacher's favourite.

- One person who always tries to get the subject on to sex.

- One person who believes they are better than everyone else in the group.

It may be useful to give a more detailed background in each case than these simple descriptions. The quiet introspective person might have parents splitting up or is being bullied by a brother. He or she might additionally be preoccupied with a cold or an injury.

These roles you can make up yourself. Here are some alternative ideas:

- One person who is always trying to flirt with the facilitator, enquiring about love, sex and the meaning of life.

- One person who is very irritable with everyone, possibly due to a drug habit, and who also spends a lot of time texting.

- One person who is using the session as a trading opportunity.

- One person who is low on confidence and tries to get others to do their work, while simultaneously looking for an opportunity to steal things.

- One person who is preoccupied with telling jokes and causing laughter – before taking offence and becoming morose.

- One person who finds it impossible to concentrate.

Remind those playing the young people that their entire aim is to set challenges for those playing facilitators. It is certainly not to defeat them or destroy the role play (which is quite easily done, given the roles outlined above…).

Exercise

Again, the aim for those running the role play is to intervene only to keep the exercise on track. If things go wrong, it may be because the 'young people' play their roles too energetically and the facilitator simply can't make headway. If this should happen, firefighting skills are probably required. It's always possible to suspend the exercise for an individual group, do a rebrief and then resume. What's important for the young people is that they should respond positively when they feel they are being dealt with effectively, and withdraw when feeling disempowered.

Evaluation

The focus in the evaluation is again on what worked, and why. Some questions:

- To what extent was the facilitator able to balance the competing claims of the individuals for attention?

- Was a sense of a group created despite the difficulties?

- Did the facilitator adapt the exercise at all so it worked for those characters?

- Did the team emerge from the process with submissions to the competition?

- Did the submissions democratically reflect the creativity of the team?

- How did the young people feel about how they were dealt with?

- What strategies did they like and not like?

- What do the results of the exercise tell us about the nature of facilitation?

An interesting point of reflection concerns how the person in charge of each team chose to deal with the actual task of redesigning the flag. One approach might be to simply get the participants to each design their own flag. A different approach would involve the team working together to make a single design between them. A particularly creative approach I've seen involved getting each participant to create one quarter of a flag, each quarter reflecting a different aspect of national life.

189

118

TRAINING

Ultimately, a lot will depend on how the facilitator managed to create relationships within the team. The issue of personalities is important. You can't change your own and it can be counterproductive to suppress those of the team around you. In respect of your own instinctive way of tackling problems, it's probably fair to say that it has to be part of the mix. There's no point trying either to be someone you're not, or hiding your own learning and teaching styles behind a mask of authority. The point is not so much to pretend to be someone else, but rather to extend as far as possible the behavioural vocabulary of your own personality.

190

Ladder of Engagement

Keith Johnstone has various exercises designed to eliminate boredom from story-making; this exercise is developed from that work. It's really about self-modelling and learning how to engage a group and keep them interested.

This could be run either by a single facilitator or two working together. The task is to describe a project to an audience of participants who will respond positively or negatively to what you are saying.

Preparation

One or two members of the group need to prepare some ideas for an imagined project. For example, the project involves making a film set in and around a local estate. Let's imagine these facilitators have to lead an initial session with a group of young unemployed people. In this, they need to animate the group with their ideas. There's only a short time available, so in this first session, several things have to be achieved. The leaders have to:

- Introduce themselves.
- Get the names of the participants.
- Outline the project.
- Explain the tasks for the day.
- Lay down any rules for sessions in terms of discipline, punctuality, swearing or behaviour which is disallowed.
- Enlist support for a project that will have challenges and difficulties ahead.

The two individual facilitators will need to discuss in advance how they are going to achieve these aims.

The rest of the group will need to clarify their roles in the exercise and determine their ages, disposition, group context, etc.

All those playing young people sit down on chairs to listen to the presentation. In contrast to the other training exercises, this time the young people cooperate initially with the presentation – unless they find themselves losing interest or getting bored. If this happens, they do one of a series of things:

- Initial disinterest or loss of focus is demonstrated by putting up a hand.

- If this is not dealt with and the participant is not brought back, he or she gets off the chair and sits on the floor.

- If this is not dealt with, the individual lies on the floor.

- If this is still not dealt with, the individual goes to sleep and starts snoring.

- If, on the other hand, the individual feels animated and engaged, this is expressed by listening intently and applauding.

- If at any point a participant is brought back into attentiveness, he or she moves back up the ladder of engagement until they're sitting attentively on the chair again.

Exercise

The challenge for the two facilitators is to achieve, as far as possible, getting everyone in the group sitting forward on their chairs and listening intently. If either takes the presentation off in the wrong direction, then it should be apparent because someone has put up a hand or sat on the floor. So that person will need some eye contact and personal acknowledgement to bring him or her back into the circle of attention.

This set of procedures can be maintained into the first exercise of the session, if it's an exercise that doesn't involve any running around. An exercise that might work would be one in which a film storyboard is created using pre-existing photographs (see game 42: *The Truth About Drugs and Crime*, page 46).

Evaluation

The evaluation should focus on why the participants took decisions to put up a hand or sit or lie on the floor. This is the time for those in role as young people to feed back exactly what was problematic or ineffective about the presentation:

- Was it to do with the relationship between the two facilitators?

- Did they work well together?
- Did they inspire the group? If so, how?
- If not, was it the vocabulary used or the project description that was off-putting?
- When a spectator started losing interest, what tactics were used to pull that person back in and were they effective?
- What was the quality of the eye contact between the facilitators and the group?
- What other tactics might have been used that weren't?
- Was there any key information about the project that was left out?

INDEX OF GAMES

KEYWORDS

NUMBERS REFER TO GAMES NOT PAGES

Abandon
34. Russian Shoemakers

Acceptance
12. Bang!
22. No, You Didn't
28. Bears are Coming, The
37. On the Bus

Affirmation
37. On the Bus
58. Priorities

Alertness
30. Zoom – Screech

Antisocial behaviour
31. Staring Competition

Anxiety
60. Gossip

Argument
67. Argument Game, The
73. Argument Room, The

Art of compromise
21. Prisoner's Dilemma
75. Taxi Ride
77. Both Want the Car
78. Blue Room, Green Room

Articulacy
24. Antiques
67. Argument Game, The
68. I'm a Celebrity Prisoner, Get Me Out of Here!
74. Community Centre
75. Taxi Ride

Assertiveness
106. Carpets by Moonlight
107. Bullying at Work
108. Taking Care of Grandpa
109. Fire Station, The
110. Talking to the School

Attentiveness
2. Football Teams
9. Numbers Game
10. Numbers Game 2
32. Word Smuggling

Audience
42. Truth About Drugs and Crime, The
50. Whose Story is True?
67. Argument Game, The
72. Chinese Mime

Awkwardness
84. Two People Meet

Balance
61. Boxing
62. Sticks
65. Fast-Food Martial Arts

Behaviour
34. Russian Shoemakers
37. On the Bus
39. Clint Eastwood
46. Behaviour of the Room, The
47. Find Your Gang
81. Three Nations
93. Old People's Home, The
101. Job Centre, The

Blindfolds
26. Vampires
51. Predicaments
66. Lightest Point of Contact
71. Minefield

Body language
4. Passing the Object
10. Numbers Game 2
50. Whose Story is True?

Bullying
107. Bullying at Work

Cliques
33. Wizards, Giants, Elves

Collaboration
36. Tug of War
37. On the Bus
38. Map of the Town
39. Clint Eastwood
40. Body Map
41. Identity Zone, The
42. Truth About Drugs and Crime, The

43. Hunting the Lion
44. Newspaper Game
52. Press-Ups
86. Blind Offers

Communication skills
67. Argument Game, The
68. I'm a Celebrity Prisoner, Get Me Out of Here!
69. Word Smuggling 2
70. Animals / Drink / Sport
71. Minefield
72. Chinese Mime
73. Argument Room, The
74. Community Centre
96. Chairs, The
97. Christmas Present, The
98. Youth Club, The
99. Untrustworthy Partner, The
100. Cold Turkey

Competitiveness
1. Name Three Times
2. Football Teams
5. Newspaper Race
6. Chairs Game, The
8. Yes / No
20. Scarf Game, The
31. Staring Competition
36. Tug of War
61. Boxing
81. Three Nations

Complementarity
23. Complete the Image

Compromise
21. Prisoner's Dilemma
75. Taxi Ride
77. Both Want the Car
78. Blue Room, Green Room
79. Wedding Funeral, The

Concentration
3. Identifying Objects
31. Staring Competition
46. Behaviour of the Room, The

Conflict
60. Gossip
75. Taxi Ride
81. Three Nations
91. Stolen Jacket, The
92. Chat-Up, The

93. Old People's Home, The
94. Forged Tickets
95. Couple Who Argue, The

Confrontation
107. Bullying at Work
113. Bully Boyfriend, The
114. Zone of Confrontation

Connectedness
36. Tug of War
37. On the Bus
43. Hunting the Lion

Contact, physical
4. Passing the Object
7. Bomb and Shield
26. Vampires
34. Russian Shoemakers
63. Shapes in the Dark
66. Lightest Point of Contact
116. Pushing

Conversation
15. Continuum
32. Word Smuggling
69. Word Smuggling 2

Cooperation
6. Chairs Game, The
26. Vampires
36. Tug of War
37. On the Bus
44. Newspaper Game
54. Name That Object
61. Boxing
62. Sticks

Coordination, hand/eye
61. Boxing
62. Sticks
65. Fast-Food Martial Arts

Coping with failure
11. Hiss and Boo
12. Bang!
21. Prisoner's Dilemma
35. Egg Game, The
97. Christmas Present, The

Crime
38. Map of the Town
42. Truth About Drugs and Crime, The
68. I'm a Celebrity Prisoner, Get Me Out of Here!

197

Crime prevention
38.   Map of the Town

Dealing with rejection
22.   No, You Didn't
94.   Forged Tickets
98.   Youth Club, The

Decoding
18.   Don, The
49.   Bandleader

Deduction
18.   Don, The
49.   Bandleader

Difference, recognition of
25.   Changeable Object
37.   On the Bus

Difference, acceptance of
37.   On the Bus
40.   Body Map
41.   Identity Zone, The

Divisions, breaking down
33.   Wizards, Giants, Elves
40.   Body Map

Drugs
38.   Map of the Town
42.   Truth About Drugs and
      Crime, The
98.   Youth Club, The
100. Cold Turkey
104. Drugs in Prison
107. Bullying at Work

Emotions, managing
39.   Clint Eastwood
76.   Jobsworth Line, The
94.   Forged Tickets
111. Broken Radio, The
112. Adult Education Class,
      The
113. Bully Boyfriend, The
114. Zone of Confrontation
115. Mistaken Identity

Energy
7.   Bomb and Shield
17.   Dog and Bone
20.   Scarf Game, The
30.   Zoom – Screech

Engagement
1.   Name Three Times
2.   Football Teams
3.   Identifying Objects
4.   Passing the Object
5.   Newspaper Race
6.   Chairs Game, The
7.   Bomb and Shield
8.   Yes / No
9.   Numbers Game
10.   Numbers Game 2
11.   Hiss and Boo
12.   Bang!
13.   Drama Nein Danke
14.   Ailments
15.   Continuum
16.   Tin-CanPulse
17.   Dog and Bone
18.   Don, The
19.   Working with Images
20.   Scarf Game, The
21.   Prisoner's Dilemma
119. Ladder of Engagement

Excitement
5.   Newspaper Race
7.   Bomb and Shield
26.   Vampires
28.   Bears are Coming, The
29.   Cat and Mouse

Failure, coping with
11.   Hiss and Boo
12.   Bang!
21.   Prisoner's Dilemma
35.   Egg Game, The
97.   Christmas Present, The

Fair play
29.   Cat and Mouse

Film
42.   Truth About Drugs and
      Crime, The

Flexibility of attitude
22.   No, You Didn't
25.   Changeable Object
67.   Argument Game, The

Focus
1.   Name Three Times
8.   Yes / No
9.   Numbers Game
10.   Numbers Game 2
16.   Tin-Can Pulse

Fun
2.   Football Teams
5.   Newspaper Race
6.   Chairs Game, The
7.   Bomb and Shield
12. Bang!
14. Ailments
17. Dog and Bone
20. Scarf Game, The
26. Vampires
27. Shoes Game
28. Bears are Coming, The
29. Cat and Mouse
30. Zoom – Screech
34. Russian Shoemakers
35. Egg Game, The

Group cohesion
49. Bandleader
50. Whose Story is True?

Holistic thinking
57. What Happened Here?
58. Priorities
59. Balloon, The

Identity
40. Body Map
41. Identity Zone, The
115. Mistaken Identity

Image
7.   Bomb and Shield
19. Working with Images
23. Complete the Image
48. Big Picture, The
63. Shapes in the Dark

Imagination
3.   Identifying Objects
25. Changeable Object
42. Truth About Drugs and
     Crime, The
64. Journeys
88. Park Bench
90. Selling

Improvisation
13. Drama Nein Danke
25. Changeable Object
39. Clint Eastwood
43. Hunting the Lion
56. Missing Character
74. Community Centre
82. Reactions
83. Following

84. Two People Meet
85. First Lines of Scenes
86. Blind Offers
87. Bridge, The
88. Park Bench
89. Two Rush In
90. Selling

Impulse management
6.   Chairs Game, The
8.   Yes / No
9.   Numbers Game
10. Numbers Game 2
12. Bang!
16. Tin-Can Pulse
17. Dog and Bone

Ingenuity
5.   Newspaper Race
21. Prisoner's Dilemma
24. Antiques
55. Obstacle Race
69. Word Smuggling 2

Interactivity
All

Kinaesthetic skills
61. Boxing
62. Sticks
63. Shapes in the Dark
64. Journeys
65. Fast-Food Martial Arts
66. Lightest Point of Contact

Learning
15. Continuum
18. Don, The
21. Prisoner's Dilemma
61. Boxing
84. Two People Meet

Listening
9.   Numbers Game
10. Numbers Game 2
32. Word Smuggling
50. Whose Story is True?
75. Taxi Ride
77. Both Want the Car
79. Wedding Funeral, The

Mediation skills
91. Stolen Jacket, The
92. Chat-Up, The
93. Old People's Home, The
94. Forged Tickets

95. Couple Who Argue, The

Memory
45. Kim's Game
46. Behaviour of the Room, The
48. Big Picture, The
72. Chinese Mime

Miming
25. Changeable Object
72. Chinese Mime

Motor skills
4. Passing the Object
62. Sticks

Movement
2. Football Teams
6. Chairs Game, The
16. Tin-Can Pulse
17. Dog and Bone
20. Scarf Game, The
28. Bears are Coming, The
29. Cat and Mouse
33. Wizards, Giants, Elves

Negativity
11. Hiss and Boo
13. Drama Nein Danke
60. Gossip
73. Argument Room, The
95. Couple Who Argue, The
107. Bullying at Work
114. Zone of Confrontation

Negotiation skills
101. Job Centre, The
102. Burger Bar, The
103. Post Office, The
104. Drugs in Prison
105. Mobile Phone Shop, The

Objects
24. Antiques
25. Changeable Object
45. Kim's Game
54. Name That Object
81. Three Nations

Observation skills
12. Bang!
23. Complete the Image
45. Kim's Game
46. Behaviour of the Room, The

47. Find Your Gang
48. Big Picture, The
49. Bandleader
50. Whose Story is True?

Outsider
6. Chairs Game, The
56. Missing Character

Pairs games
22. No, You Didn't
61. Boxing
64. Journeys
69. Word Smuggling 2
85. First Lines of Scenes

Performance skills
82. Reactions
83. Following
84. Two People Meet
85. First Lines of Scenes
86. Blind Offers
87. Bridge, The
88. Park Bench
89. Two Rush In
90. Selling

Photos
19. Working with Images
42. Truth About Drugs and Crime, The
48. Big Picture, The

Physical awareness
20. Scarf Game, The
61. Boxing
62. Sticks
63. Shapes in the Dark
64. Journeys
65. Fast-Food Martial Arts
66. Lightest Point of Contact

Physical contact
4. Passing the Object
7. Bomb and Shield
26. Vampires
34. Russian Shoemakers
63. Shapes in the Dark
66. Lightest Point of Contact
116. Pushing

Physical skills
61. Boxing
62. Sticks
65. Fast-Food Martial Arts

Play

22. No, You Didn't
23. Complete the Image
24. Antiques
25. Changeable Object
26. Vampires
27. Shoes Game
28. Bears are Coming, The
29. Cat and Mouse
30. Zoom – Screech
31. Staring Competition
32. Word Smuggling
33. Wizards, Giants, Elves
34. Russian Shoemakers
35. Egg Game, The

Playfulness

7. Bomb and Shield
27. Shoes Game

Pressure, coping with

70. Animals / Drink / Sport
91. Stolen Jacket, The
102. Burger Bar, The
103. Post Office, The
106. Carpets by Moonlight

Prison

21. Prisoner's Dilemma
67. Argument Game, The
68. I'm a Celebrity Prisoner, Get Me Out of Here!
104. Drugs in Prison
111. Broken Radio, The
114. Zone of Confrontation

Problem-solving

38. Map of the Town
51. Predicaments
52. Press-Ups
53. Shortest Time Possible
54. Name That Object
55. Obstacle Race
56. Missing Character
57. What Happened Here?
58. Priorities
59. Balloon, The
60. Gossip
44. Newspaper Game
75. Taxi Ride
76. Jobsworth Line, The
77. Both Want the Car
78. Blue Room, Green Room
79. Wedding Funeral, The
80. Zoom – Screech

Quickness of mind

1. Name Three Times
2. Football Teams
8. Yes / No
9. Numbers Game
10. Numbers Game 2
12. Bang!
35. Egg Game, The

Reasoning skills

11. Hiss and Boo
51. Predicaments
52. Press-Ups
53. Shortest Time Possible
54. Name That Object
55. Obstacle Race
56. Missing Character
57. What Happened Here?
58. Priorities
59. Balloon, The
60. Gossip
68. I'm a Celebrity Prisoner, Get Me Out of Here!
73. Argument Room, The
104. Drugs in Prison
111. Broken Radio, The
115. Mistaken Identity

Relationships

42. Truth About Drugs and Crime, The
57. What Happened Here?
58. Priorities
77. Both Want the Car
93. Old People's Home, The
95. Couple Who Argue, The
97. Christmas Present, The
99. Untrustworthy Partner, The
101. Job Centre, The
102. Burger Bar, The
108. Taking Care of Grandpa
111. Broken Radio, The
113. Bully Boyfriend, The

Release

2. Football Teams
5. Newspaper Race
6. Chairs Game, The
7. Bomb and Shield
26. Vampires
29. Cat and Mouse
34. Russian Shoemakers

Rejection, dealing with
22. No, You Didn't

Rhythm
27. Shoes Game
49. Bandleader

Risk
81. Three Nations
102. Burger Bar, The

Running
6. Chairs Game, The
7. Bomb and Shield
17. Dog and Bone
20. Scarf Game, The

Self-analysis
41. Identity Zone, The

Self-discipline
54. Name That Object
87. Bridge, The

Self-observation
6. Chairs Game, The

Sensitivity
3. Identifying Objects
66. Lightest Point of Contact

Skills, behavioural
91. Stolen Jacket, The
92. Chat-Up, The
93. Old People's Home, The
94. Forged Tickets
95. Couple Who Argue, The
96. Chairs, The
97. Christmas Present, The
98. Youth Club, The
99. Untrustworthy Partner, The
100. Cold Turkey
101. Job Centre, The
102. Burger Bar, The
103. Post Office, The
104. Drugs in Prison
105. Mobile Phone Shop, The
106. Carpets by Moonlight
107. Bullying at Work
108. Taking Care of Grandpa
109. Fire Station, The
110. Talking to the School
111. Broken Radio, The
112. Adult Education Class, The

113. Bully Boyfriend, The
114. Zone of Confrontation
115. Mistaken Identity

Skills, communication
67. Argument Game, The
68. I'm a Celebrity Prisoner, Get Me Out of Here!
69. Word Smuggling 2
70. Animals / Drink / Sport
71. Minefield
72. Chinese Mime
73. Argument Room, The
74. Community Centre
96. Chairs, The
97. Christmas Present, The
98. Youth Club, The
99. Untrustworthy Partner, The
100. Cold Turkey

Skills, mediation
91. Stolen Jacket, The
92. Chat-Up, The
93. Old People's Home, The
94. Forged Tickets
95. Couple Who Argue, The

Skills, negotiation
101. Job Centre, The
102. Burger Bar, The
103. Post Office, The
104. Drugs in Prison
105. Mobile Phone Shop, The

Skills, reasoning
11. Hiss and Boo
51. Predicaments
52. Press-Ups
53. Shortest Time Possible
54. Name That Object
55. Obstacle Race
56. Missing Character
57. What Happened Here?
58. Priorities
59. Balloon, The
60. Gossip
68. I'm a Celebrity Prisoner, Get Me Out of Here!
73. Argument Room, The
104. Drugs in Prison
111. Broken Radio, The
115. Mistaken Identity

Skills, observation

12. Bang!
23. Complete the Image
45. Kim's Game
46. Behaviour of the Room, The
47. Find Your Gang
48. Big Picture, The
49. Bandleader
50. Whose Story is True?

Skills, kinaesthetic

61. Boxing
62. Sticks
63. Shapes in the Dark
64. Journeys
65. Fast-Food Martial Arts
66. Lightest Point of Contact

Skills, performance

82. Reactions
83. Following
84. Two People Meet
85. First Lines of Scenes
86. Blind Offers
87. Bridge, The
88. Park Bench
89. Two Rush In
90. Selling

Skills, problem-solving

38. Map of the Town
51. Predicaments
52. Press-Ups
53. Shortest Time Possible
54. Name That Object
55. Obstacle Race
56. Missing Character
57. What Happened Here?
58. Priorities
59. Balloon, The
60. Gossip
44. Newspaper Game
75. Taxi Ride
76. Jobsworth Line, The
77. Both Want the Car
78. Blue Room, Green Room
79. Wedding Funeral, The
80. Drunk on the Bus

Speed of reaction

12. Bang!
16. Tin-Can Pulse
17. Dog and Bone

Spontaneity

6. Chairs Game, The
82. Reactions
84. Two People Meet

Story-making

19. Working with Images
42. Truth About Drugs and Crime, The

Storytelling

13. Drama Nein Danke
14. Ailments
42. Truth About Drugs and Crime, The
50. Whose Story is True?
72. Chinese Mime
89. Two Rush In

Teamwork

5. Newspaper Race
6. Chairs Game, The
13. Drama Nein Danke
16. Tin-Can Pulse
21. Prisoner's Dilemma
27. Shoes Game
30. Zoom – Screech
36. Tug of War
45. Kim's Game
53. Shortest Time Possible
55. Obstacle Race
62. Sticks
66. Lightest Point of Contact
81. Three Nations
90. Selling

Tension, dramatic

31. Staring Competition
36. Tug of War
7. Bomb and Shield
84. Two People Meet

Thinking, lateral

44. Newspaper Game
53. Shortest Time Possible
87. Bridge, The

Thinking skills

11. Hiss and Boo
51. Predicaments
52. Press-Ups
53. Shortest Time Possible
54. Name That Object
55. Obstacle Race
56. Missing Character
57. What Happened Here?

58. Priorities
59. Balloon, The
60. Gossip
68. I'm a Celebrity Prisoner,
     Get Me Out of Here!
73. Argument Room, The
104. Drugs in Prison
111. Broken Radio, The
115. Mistaken Identity

Thoughtfulness
21. Prisoner's Dilemma
57. What Happened Here?
58. Priorities
59. Balloon, The

Time management
53. Shortest Time Possible
58. Priorities

Touch
4. Passing the Object
7. Bomb and Shield
26. Vampires
34. Russian Shoemakers
63. Shapes in the Dark
66. Lightest Point of Contact
116. Pushing

Trust
64. Journeys
99. Untrustworthy Partner,
     The

Verbal communication
8. Yes / No
22. No, You Didn't
32. Word Smuggling
67. Argument Game, The
68. I'm a Celebrity Prisoner,
     Get Me Out of Here!
69. Word Smuggling 2
70. Animals / Drink / Sport
71. Minefield
72. Chinese Mime
73. Argument Room, The
74. Community Centre

Vocabulary
32. Word Smuggling
117. Brilliant / Shit

ALPHABETICAL LIST

NUMBERS REFER TO GAMES NOT PAGES

112. Adult Education Class, The
14. Ailments
70. Animals / Drink / Sport
24. Antiques
67. Argument Game, The
73. Argument Room, The
59. Balloon, The
49. Bandleader
12. Bang!
28. Bears are Coming, The
46. Behaviour of the Room, The
48. Big Picture, The
86. Blind Offers
78. Blue Room, Green Room
40. Body Map
7. Bomb and Shield
77. Both Want the Car
61. Boxing
87. Bridge, The
117. Brilliant / Shit
111. Broken Radio, The
113. Bully Boyfriend, The
107. Bullying at Work
102. Burger Bar, The
106. Carpets by Moonlight
29. Cat and Mouse
96. Chairs, The
6. Chairs Game, The
25. Changeable Object
92. Chat-Up, The
72. Chinese Mime
97. Christmas Present, The
39. Clint Eastwood
100. Cold Turkey
74. Community Centre
23. Complete the Image
15. Continuum
95. Couple Who Argue, The
17. Dog and Bone
18. Don, The
13. Drama Nein Danke
104. Drugs in Prison
80. Drunk on the Bus
35. Egg Game, The
65. Fast-Food Martial Arts
47. Find Your Gang
109. Fire Station, The
85. First Line of Scenes
83. Following
2. Football Teams

94. Forged Tickets
60. Gossip
11. Hiss and Boo
43. Hunting the Lion
68. I'm a Celebrity Prisoner, Get Me Out of Here!
3. Identifying Objects
41. Identity Zone, The
101. Job Centre, The
76. Jobsworth Line, The
64. Journeys
45. Kim's Game
119. Ladder of Engagement
66. Lightest Point of Contact
38. Map of the Town
71. Minefield
56. Missing Character
115. Mistaken Identity
105. Mobile Phone Shop, The
54. Name That Object
1. Name Three Times
118. New National Flag, A
44. Newspaper Game
5. Newspaper Race
22. No, You Didn't
9. Numbers Game
10. Numbers Game 2
55. Obstacle Race
93. Old People's Home, The
37. On the Bus
88. Park Bench
4. Passing the Object
103. Post Office, The
51. Predicaments
52. Press-Ups
58. Priorities
21. Prisoner's Dilemma
116. Pushing
82. Reactions
34. Russian Shoemakers
20. Scarf Game, The
90. Selling
63. Shapes in the Dark
27. Shoes Game
53. Shortest Time Possible
31. Staring Competition
62. Sticks
91. Stolen Jacket, The
108. Taking Care of Grandpa
110. Talking to the School
75. Taxi Ride
81. Three Nations

16. Tin-Can Pulse
42. Truth About Drugs and Crime, The
36. Tug of War
84. Two People Meet
89. Two Rush In
99. Untrustworthy Partner, The
26. Vampires
79. Wedding Funeral, The

57. What Happened Here?
50. Whose Story is True?
33. Wizards, Giants, Elves
32. Word Smuggling
69. Word Smuggling 2
19. Working with Images
8. Yes / No
98. Youth Club, The
114. Zone of Confrontation
30. Zoom – Screech

NOTES

NOTES

NOTES

NOTES